THE FULL
GOSPEL

Reclaiming
the Gospel
of the Kingdom!

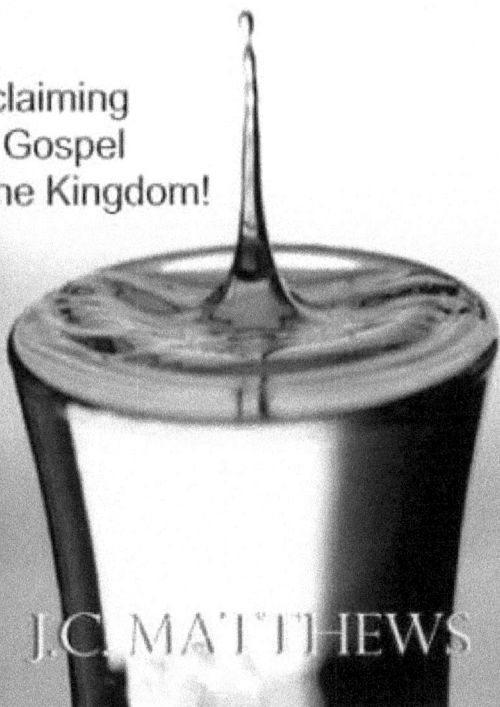

J.C. MATTHEWS

FULL GOSPEL

J.C. Matthews

The FULL Gospel

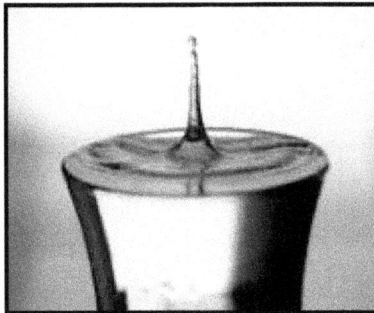

Reclaiming the Gospel of the Kingdom

REIGN Worldwide Publication
A REIGN Worldwide Inc,
www.reignworldwide.com

FULL GOSPEL

The FULL Gospel: Reclaiming the Gospel of the Kingdom

ISBN – 0-9792554-7-3
ISBN – 978-0-9792554-7-2

© 2010 REIGN Worldwide, Inc.

REIGN Worldwide Publications
P.O. Box 1083
Keller, Texas 76244

For more information about REIGN Worldwide, Inc. and its products call 1-888-800-4896 or visit www.reignworldwide.org.

FULL GOSPEL

Table of Contents

FULL GOSPEL

The FULL Gospel

Reclaiming the Gospel of the Kingdom

FULL GOSPEL

The Gospel

The Gospel

The impetus for this book was actually birthed from a conversation I had with a pastor from India who flew to Dallas to attend our Kingdom Consciousness Workshop. During the workshop, while I was teaching, I notice tears streaming down the pastor's face. At the conclusion of the workshop, the pastor asked if we could talk a little about what I taught during the workshop. I agreed and we met for dinner. During our dinner conversation I asked the pastor why he was crying during the teaching. His answer shocked me, while at the same time opened my eyes to a major problem in what we have been proclaiming and sharing as the *gospel*.

The pastor went on to explain; that the reason he cried during the teaching was that he realized that he had finally found the answer to several questions concerning the Christian walk that he could not answer that came from his congregation and those he encountered when trying to evangelize the unbeliever in his home country. He explained that in India, Christianity is referred to as the *"poor man's religion"*. He said that this is due to the vast majority of the Christian missionaries' evangelism efforts having been concentrated on the poor in his country to the exclusion of the other segments of their society. The missionary taught and delivered to them the *gospel of salvation;* which gave them hope of one day (after they've died) escaping the poverty, misery and suffering of their day to day lives, but gave them very little hope or instruction on what the implications of their salvation was for the remainder of their lives here and now. As a result, several negative results occurred from this narrow perspective of the Gospel. One of the negative results was that the more affluent segments of their society continued to practice their native religions, which were primarily Muslim and other forms of idol worship, while the poorest segments increasingly grew Christian. As a result, the more affluent members of their society resisted becoming Christian because to do so was considered a demotion in their society.

I asked the pastor, if had he personally tried to evangelize the more affluent, and if so, what was his experience? He indicated that he had attempted to do so, but found it very difficult for several reasons: (1) the more affluent had no real physical needs that he could meet in order to create the opportunity to evangelize them, and (2) he could not offer them the prospect of eternal life after their physical death because their current religion already promised them the hope of paradise or a *better life* in the life to come.

Therefore, the salvation only gospel had no real impact or influence upon them. It was another option amongst many that appeared to only offer a demotion in their society, poverty and a hope of life after their physical death, which they already had.

He went on to say that he also experienced difficulty in ministering to his own congregation due to the daily hardships they faced; and the only real hope they had was dying and going to heaven. Therefore, many converts often fell back into their prior religions because the Gospel he was teaching them appeared to lack the ability to impact or make a difference in the life they still had left to live.

This pastor looked me in the eyes and said:

"This is the reason I cried when hearing you teach the message of the Kingdom! I had never heard *this gospel* before, but there it was throughout the Bible. It was

15

there all the time!" He went on to say:
"I saw in the Bible Jesus Himself
teaching and demonstrating the
Kingdom with power. He was not weak.
He was a King, who was a descendent of
kings, and brought a kingdom with Him.
His followers continued in the same
power as they advanced the Kingdom of
God throughout the New Testament.
This gospel is so powerful. It gives me
the ability to speak hope and
empowerment into the lives of the
people. It is the answer I'd been seeking
concerning God's will for our lives in *this*
lifetime."

He went on to explain:

"This will enable me to take the Gospel
message to the more affluent because
they will be more inclined to associate
themselves with a King; not the pauper

that many of the missionaries and bible schools portrayed Jesus as being".

This pastor concluded our conversation by stating:

"This gospel of the Kingdom could not only reach another class of people for Christ, but could actually overcome many of the societal barriers, due to Christianity being perceived as a "poor man's religion", and bring the classes together."

For the rest of the evening he talked of the possibilities that the Gospel of the Kingdom could create in his country. As we were leaving, he hugged me and said that he was excited about going back to India and thanked me for sharing the *rest of the gospel* with him.

The Rest of the Gospel

Later that night, as I reflected on our conversation, I could not get the pastor's comment concerning *"the rest of the gospel"* out of my mind. Was this an isolated incident confined to a distant corner of the world, or was this pastor's experience representative of a larger problem prevailing throughout the body of Christ? As I talked to others pastors and believers, both domestically and abroad, I discovered that my pastor friend from India experience was not an exception. Those I spoke to were intimately acquainted with the gospel of salvation, but not much more. When I suggested that the salvation message was not Jesus' central message and that there was a *greater* purpose and message that Jesus taught and delivered to the church they appeared disturbed.

Many of them asked: "What could be greater than a soul's salvation? I answered: "What's greater is the *purpose* for which one's soul is saved". I explained that the gospel of salvation is the means by which we are introduced and initiated into a greater purpose and revelation that directly impacts our lives here on earth, as well as God's ultimate plan for mankind for all of eternity. The greater purpose than salvation itself is its purpose – the Kingdom! We are saved so that we qualify for entrance into God's Kingdom which is only comprised of spiritual sons. The salvation or born again experience is not the culmination, but the initiation or beginning or our realizing God's purpose for us in the earth.

The Kingdom is what all of humanity is seeking and striving to experience and receive since it lost the Kingdom in the Garden. It is the provision and good news that man is desperately seeking to answer his most basic needs:

provision, protection and purpose. It is that which my pastor friend referred to as *"the rest of the gospel"* or the *"Full Gospel"*. The Full Gospel, not only includes our soul's salvation, but provides us with the means to experience the restoration of all that was lost by man in the Garden!

The Good News

When anyone speaks of "The Gospels" most people in the Body of Christ immediately think of the first 4 books of the New Testament: *Matthew, Mark, Luke and John*. These four books contain the account of the birth, life, death and resurrection of Jesus Christ, who is the focus of the Gospels. However, these 4 books are really the beginning, not the culmination, of the revelation Christ and the work He came to finish. Jesus' work was one of deliverance and restoration of that which was lost (Luke 19:10). Every one of the gospels contribute to the revelation of God's goodness toward man in making provision for the restoration of that which He declared as "good" and "very good" when He created man and placed him in the earth. This restoration is the *"good news"* that Jesus came to demonstrate, proclaim and again deliver to mankind.

"The Gospels"

I must first make it clear, that when I mention the word "gospel" or "gospels" I am not referring to any non or extra-canonical books that have been recently coined as "gospels" such as: "The Gospel of Thomas", "The Gospel of Peter", "The Gospel of James", "The Gospel of Philipp" and even "The Gospel of Judas". These books are outside of the scope of our subject and are not referred to when I speak of "the Gospels".

When I speak of "the Gospels", "the rest of the Gospels" or the "Full Gospel", I am referring to the whole of the message and revelation, given by God to His people, for the purpose of enabling man to experience the restoration of the fullness that God gave him in the Garden, and all that the finished work of Christ purchased and delivered to man.

To confine the Gospels to the books written by Matthew, Mark, Luke and John would be short-sighted and would deprive the church of the Full revelation of the Gospel, or good news, that God intends for man to receive. The entire Bible must be utilized in order to determine what God considers "good news" as it pertains to man.

Gospels

Throughout the books of the New Testament we are introduced to various messages that the writer describes as being *gospel*, such as: *"The gospel of the kingdom"*, *"the gospel of God"*, *"the gospel of His Son"*, *"the gospel of Christ"*, *"Christ's gospel"*, *"the gospel of peace"*, *"gospel of your salvation"* and even *"the mystery of the gospel"*. All of these *gospels* carry a unique revelation and insight of God's goodness and restorative plan for mankind.

To gain a better understanding of why there are so many descriptors for the gospel, we must first define what is meant when we say the word *"gospel"*. To begin, the word *"gospel"* is not a religious term. The word *"gospel"* literally means *"good speak"* or *"to speak or bring good news"*. It is a message that brings *good news*. Religiously, we have confined and defined this good news mean the communication of a religious message whose objective it is to bring the lost to a saving knowledge of Jesus Christ. Although, this is an important *component* of the "good news" or "gospel" it by no means is its totality. As a matter of fact, when considering the content of the vast majority of Jesus' public teaching, as found in the four Gospels, the salvation message comprises a very small percentage of His teachings.

If we were to examine the Bible to determine what it declares as "gospel" we would discover that the word transcends the four New Testament books and really is a descriptive of the Bible as a whole. In Galatians 3:8, Paul says that God delivered the *"gospel"* to Abraham more than 2000 years before Christ or the events recorded in Matthew, Mark, Luke and John. Specifically, he says:

> *"And the Scripture, foreseeing that God would justify the Gentiles by faith, preached the gospel to Abraham beforehand, saying, "In you all the nations shall be blessed."*

The Bible calls what God proclaimed to Abraham as "the gospel". This gospel that God declared to Abraham told of His plan to bless man, through Abraham, and again make available to mankind

24

a relationship with Him based on the premises of faith.

"Very Good"

In Genesis chapter 1 God declares *7 times* that what He gave man *"is good"*! As a matter of fact, God looks back over what He prepared for man and concludes, not only is it *good*, but that it is *"very good"* (verse 31). God's goodness was so thorough and all encompassing, that man neither knew what it meant to *be in want of anything*, nor did he know what *evil* was. It was literally *"Heaven on earth"!* This was the *good news* God declared in the very first chapter of the Bible for man. This was *"God's gospel"* for mankind! This is important point to remember, because any true gospel must emphasis: (1) God's goodness, (2) Deliverance from the consequences of the curse, (3) Restoration of the Garden environment, AND

(4) Restoration of man's relationship with God and the earth.

Restoration is the decisive and primary principle of any gospel. Man, when he fell, lost his relationship with God, his Source, and the ground or earth. Earth was cursed for man's sake and instructed to withhold from him what he needs from it until man invests toil and sweat. This was not God's original plan but a consequence of sin and His judgment of it. Therefore, in order for a message to qualify as being good news it must necessarily address the restoration of God's order in the earth. If a message does not contain the essential element of restoration of this order it is incomplete, and falls short of being *good news* from God's perspective.

Any belief system, doctrine or gospel that denies, distorts or diminishes the manifold goodness of God toward man is not a gospel at all.

"Re"

The key to identifying and understanding the presence of a true and full Gospel is by gaining an appreciation for the prefix *"re"*. The prefix *"re"* is a road sign which directs our attention to a previous point in time or condition that the current action is addressing or related to. When we read the New Testament, especially as it applies to our theology and understanding of Jesus' ministry, we are consistently confronted with this prefix "re" because it is informing us that the present act is in response to prior condition. Therefore, we are told that we must *repent* and be *reborn, reconciled, resurrected, redeemed* and *restored*.

All of these words play a significant role in the constitution of what God considers to be the Full Gospel. Again, any doctrine or gospel does not contain as its foundation this message of restoration, it is not a gospel. The Gospel is the restoration of God's goodness toward man. If it does not *replace, redeem, reconcile, or resurrect* what man lost, it cannot truly be restoration, and therefore cannot be a true Gospel!

God's Purpose - Goodness

Despite all the goodness God showered upon man, Satan was able to entice him to forsake it for the knowledge the knowledge of what the Bible calls "evil". Specifically,

> *"Then the serpent said to the woman, "You will not surely die."For God knows that in the day you eat of it your eyes will be opened, and you will be like God, knowing good and evil" (Genesis 3:4-5).*

This first recorded conversation of Satan with man sheds light on how His point of attack and purpose in his attack of man. Satan initial attack on man was based upon his perception and understanding of God and His Word. His focus and method have not changed. He uses still attempts to pervert what God has given man to cause separation and division. He has used man's interpretation of God's Word, doctrine and the religious traditions of men to cause division amongst the body of Christ and in man's relationship with God. Today, there are more than 38,000 Christian denominations in the world each divided on their interpretation of God's word and what they believe to be the true gospel.

As a foundational statement, we must confess and possess a conviction that God is first and foremost good. God is good, all the time! This is what Satan attempts to obscure from man has he goes about to separate man from his Source. As witness in the fall of man, Satan will always attack, distort and try to obscure God's goodness and pervert his character in the mind of man. Secondly, he will use man's lack of knowledge and understanding of God's Word and character to cause separation between God and man.

Thirdly, he always engages man's intellect (and desire for increased knowledge) to cause him to question God and contend with the wisdom and true knowledge of God.

This is the essence of demonically inspired doctrine. No matter how eloquent, articulate, intelligent or rational a doctrine may sound; if it imputes to God character any act or motivation that is not inherently benevolent, loving, generous, compassionate and good – it is a doctrine whose origin can be found in Satan himself. Satan's primary objective is to cause man to *distrust* God and ultimately separate him from His Source, causing man to be susceptible, and in many respects, subject to his influences. Man enjoyed perfect *provision, protection* and *fulfillment of purpose* in God's Kingdom as long as he maintained his:

(1) Allegiances to God
(2) Respect of God's laws, and
(3) Respect for the things of God (or God's property).

When man allowed Satan to pervert his perspective of God and received the devil's doctrine, he lost his right to God's provision and protection, thereby frustrating his ability to fulfill his purpose in the earth. This is what man lost when Satan convinced him that God was selfishly withholding equality with Him from man. He caused man to become suspicious of God's motivations and overlook all of God's generosity. Satan knew that man was already equal with God (as it relates to the earth), by his being created in God's very likeness and image and having been given dominion over the earth, except for the tree – the tree of the knowledge of good and evil. By perverting man's perception of God's nature, feeding upon man's intellectual desire for knowledge, and taking advantage of his lack of understanding of God's Word, Satan was able to cause man to forfeit all that God had given him for the knowledge of evil.

Despite the fact that man lived in absolute abundance, he yielded to the enemy's accusations concerning God's nature and motivations, causing him to lose his relationship with his Source as well as his place in God's Kingdom.

Another Gospel

The Apostle Paul was well aware of the Satan's focus upon God's word in an effort to contaminate what man receives as doctrine or the Gospel. This is why he was so diligent in warning the churches about perverted doctrine that is the product of men's intellect, traditions and demons. Specifically, he wrote to the church at Galatia and stated:

> "I marvel that you are turning away so soon from Him who called you in the grace of Christ, to a different gospel, [7] which is not another; but there are some who trouble you and want to pervert the gospel of Christ. But even if we, or an angel from heaven, preach any other gospel to you

than what we have preached to you, let
him be accursed. As we have said before,
so now I say again, if anyone preaches any
other gospel to you than what you have
received, let him be accursed" (Gal.1:6-9).

In addition, he wrote to the church at Corinth,
likewise warning them not to entertain any
ideology, thoughts or imaginations that are
abrasive to God's goodness and the true
knowledge of God, as delivered to them by him.
Paul says that this is an attack against the
church and God's Kingdom, and must be handled
as such. Specifically, he warns:

" [Inasmuch as we] refute <u>arguments</u> and
<u>theories</u> and <u>reasonings</u> and every proud
and lofty thing that sets itself up <u>against</u>
<u>the [true] knowledge of God</u>; and we lead
every <u>thought</u> and <u>purpose</u> away captive
into the obedience of Christ (the Messiah,
the Anointed One)."(2 Cor 10:5, AMP)
(underline added).

The objective of these destructive ideologies,
doctrines and arguments is the separation of man
from the true knowledge of God, and amongst one

another. If we were to look at the landscape of the Body of Christ today, it could be said that this method of attack has been very effective. As mentioned earlier, there are more than 38,000 different Christian denominations across the world today. This number grows each year. Sunday, the day on which the Church meets, is still the most segregated day of the week. The true knowledge and nature of God is gradually being replaced with an agnostic and intellectual gospel where the righteous standards of God are being replaced with politically correct ideologies; while the very things Christ died to redeem us from are being claimed by believers as virtues, lessons from God, and His will for their lives. The Gospel that we are proclaiming is not what God perceives as good news; neither is it the good news Christ delivered to us as the Gospel. When man fell in the Garden, he did not lose a religion; he lost a government – a kingdom. When Jesus declared that upon this rock He would build His church, He was not referring to a religious institution, but an agency by which the government (Kingdom) of God would be advanced throughout the world. Man's religion cannot prevail against the gates or power of hell; only the power of God can do this! Christ came to deliver a Gospel of deliverance and restoration! You can only be restored in that which you once possessed. He did not come to restore or to create a religion because God never gave man a religion. Christ came to reestablish God's government in the earth and a relationship with a redeemed mankind.

Christ came to restore what man lost, and to declare that which was lost, is now here and available to man - again. This is the good news Christ delivered to men: *Repent, change and transform your minds and way of thinking, for God's Kingdom has been restored in the earth and is available to all who wish to enter.* Now that's good news!

The Gospel of Salvation

The Gospel of Salvation

hen speaking of *the gospel*, most people automatically assume that the speaker is referring to the *gospel of salvation* or the first four books of the New Testament (Matthew, Mark Luke and John). As a matter of fact, if we were to ask people what was Jesus primary message and ministry was they would more than likely respond: *"To save the lost"*. This answer would not be *incorrect*; however it would definitely be *incomplete*.

What if I were to suggest that Jesus never taught salvation as Gospel? Would this shock you? It should. The reason it would be shocking is because we have been taught that this was Jesus primary reason for coming – *To save they that are lost.* As we take a look at scripture, we will discover that Jesus did not say He came to save the lost, but points to His purpose the very object for which men are saved – *the Kingdom!*

In the Gospel of Luke, Jesus plainly tells us His purpose for coming is not to preach a Gospel of salvation, but to preach the good news of the return of God's Kingdom in the earth. Specifically, He says;

> *"I must preach the kingdom of God to the other cities also, because for this purpose I have been sent" (Luke 4:43).*

When Pilate asked Jesus about His identity and purpose, Jesus responded:

> *"You say rightly that I am a king. For this cause I was born, and for this cause I have come into the world ..."* *(John 18:37).*

This declaration by Jesus, of His identity and purpose, is confirmation of what the prophets foretold as the Christ's purpose for coming into the world. Specifically, the prophet Isaiah declared:

> *"For unto us a Child is born, Unto us a Son is given; And the government will be upon His shoulder. And His name will be called Wonderful, Counselor, Mighty God, Everlasting Father, Prince of Peace. Of the increase of His government and peace There will be no end, Upon the throne of David and over His kingdom, To order it and establish it with judgment and justice From that time forward, even forever"* (Isaiah 9:6-7).

Jesus came to establish and order an eternal government called the Kingdom.

The only record we have of Jesus uttering the word *"salvation"* is found only twice in the Gospels, once at Luke 19:9 and again at John 4:22. Even more interesting is the fact that Jesus only spoke of being *"born again"* once in the Gospel of John (see John 3:3, 7). Each conversation in which Jesus spoke of salvation or

being born again took place in private, on an
individual basis and in response to the
individuals question or misunderstanding
concerning how to obtain a relationship with God
or entrance into His Kingdom.

In comparison to the above, the circumstances in
which Jesus taught on the Kingdom are very
different than those in which He spoke of
salvation. If you were to look at the context in
which Jesus spoke of the Kingdom, you would
discover that they are almost exclusively to large
gatherings and initiated by Jesus. This was
Jesus' primary public message. Jesus dedicated
entire chapters within the Gospels to teaching
exclusively on the Kingdom (see Matthew 13).

Jesus uttered the word "kingdom" over 115 times
in the Gospels, in comparison to His mentioning
salvation twice and the words *"born again"* once.
If you were to get a copy of the New Testament,
close your eyes and randomly select one of its

pages; there is a high likelihood that on either of the two pages you opened, you would discover either a direct or indirect reference to the Kingdom.

It is difficult to understand how these isolated statements, concerning salvation and being born again, could grow into a doctrine that dominates the church's efforts, focus and teachings to the exclusion of Jesus' primary teaching – the Kingdom. However, believers today, including leadership, have received very little, if any, instruction on the Kingdom. It is sad to say that the vast majority of bible colleges, churches, seminaries and parachurch organization do not offer, or require, a single course on the Kingdom for graduation! However, each one of these organizations states as their purposes the effective equipping of their members and students for ministry and competent declaration of the Gospel. This is in the face of the fact that Kingdom was Jesus' primary message.

The salvation message certainly is an important component of the Gospel message, however, it comprises a very small percentage of the Full Gospel Jesus taught and delivered to the church. To limit and concentrate the Gospel's message to salvation alone is to limit the Gospels intended impact and deprive it of the revelation of its intended object – the Kingdom.

Salvation

Let me start by stating that the salvation message is absolutely necessary. It is an indispensible *element* of the good news God for man in the earth. If we were to truly understand the message of salvation, it is much more expansive than the traditional and religious understanding of what is meant when we declare that we're saved. The church's focus, and primary message, has become the salvation of our *souls,* when the salvation Jesus

43

demonstrated and taught encompassed every aspect of man's life: mind, body and spirit.

The principle upon with salvation is premised is *deliverance* and *restoration* from the effects of sin, the curse and the fall. The original *Gospel of Salvation* was proclaimed by God in Genesis 3:15 in response to man's fall, when He promised:

> *"I will put enmity between you and the woman, and between your offspring and hers; he will crush your head, and you will strike his heel" (NIV).*

God promised that He would send a *deliverer* through the "Seed" of the woman who would destroy and undo what Satan gained through deception. We know that this *Deliverer, or Seed,* is Jesus Christ the Messiah. The Bible says that:

> *"For this purpose the Son of God was manifested, that He might destroy the works of the devil" (1John 3:8b).*

Therefore, whatever constitutes the "work" of Satan, Jesus delivered and saved us from. Jesus destroyed and undid the damage that sin, the fall and the curse inflicted upon man. Some of the "*works of the devil*" that Jesus delivered man from was: (1) spiritual death and separation from God, (2) the requirement that man to toil and sweat for his needs to be met, and (3) sickness in man's body, mind and spirit. All of the above were benefits man enjoyed prior to losing his place in God's Kingdom.

The restoration of these benefits for those who would enter God's Kingdom was the good news Jesus proclaimed as being available to man again. This aspect of deliverance, restoration *and* salvation are seen when Paul says:

> *"He has delivered us from the power of darkness and conveyed us into the kingdom of the Son of His love"*
> *(Colossians 1:13)*

Jesus and the Message of Salvation

By taking a closer look at the instances in which Jesus speaks of *salvation* or of being *born again*, we can gain a clearer understanding of what He meant when He spoke of salvation. We will discover that our soul's salvation was never was never intended to be the totality or culmination of the"gospel" but the introduction into a greater reality called the Kingdom.

John 3:3-6

In John chapter 3, a Pharisee named Nicodemus visits Jesus in the middle of the night, where He explains to him:

> *"Most assuredly, I say to you, unless one is born again, he cannot see the kingdom of God." Nicodemus said to Him, "How can a man be born when he is old? Can he enter a second time into his mother's womb and be born?" Jesus answered, "Most assuredly, I say to*

*you, unless one is born of water and the
Spirit, he cannot enter the kingdom of
God."That which is born of the flesh is
flesh and that which is born of the
Spirit is spirit" (John 3:3-6).*

Jesus message to Nicodemus was not one of
salvation, but one of instruction concerning how
we are to enter the Kingdom of God. To
understand the reason for Jesus directing this
conversation to *how,* or by what means, one
enters the Kingdom of God, we must understand
the context. To begin Nicodemus was a Pharisee.
The Pharisees believed their strict adherence to
the Law (works) and their being descendants of
Abraham (flesh) was their key to entrance into
God's Kingdom. In Matthew chapter 3, John the
Baptist warned the Pharisees of the error in their
understanding when he said:

*"In those days John the Baptist came
preaching in the wilderness of Judea, and
saying, "Repent, for the kingdom of
heaven is at hand!" ... 'But when he saw
many of the Pharisees and Sadducees
coming to his baptism, he said to them,*

> *"Brood of vipers! Who warned you to flee*
> *from the wrath to come? Therefore bear*
> *fruits worthy of repentance, and do not*
> *think to say to yourselves, 'We have*
> *Abraham as our father.' For I say to you*
> *that God is able to raise up children to*
> *Abraham from these stones"*
> *(Matthew 3:1-3, 7-9).*

This is why Jesus interrupts Nicodemus and directly addresses this error concerning how we are to enter the Kingdom of God. It is not based on works (keeping of the Law) nor of the flesh (their relationship to Abraham), but through faith and the work of the Holy Spirit. Again, Jesus' primary purpose in speaking to Nicodemus was not to establish being born again as the Gospel message, but to correct his misunderstanding of how one enters the object of our being born again – *God's Kingdom!*

John 4:7-27

In John 4, Jesus is speaking with a Samaritan woman He met at the well. Specifically He says:

"Jesus said to her, "Woman, believe Me, the hour is coming when you will neither on this mountain, nor in Jerusalem, worship the Father. "You worship what you do not know; we know what we worship, for salvation is of the Jews. "But the hour is coming, and now is, when the true worshipers will worship the Father in spirit and truth; for the Father is seeking such to worship Him."God is Spirit, and those who worship Him must worship in spirit and truth" (John 4:21-24).

Jesus asks the woman for a drink of water, and she begins to speak of the religious and societal restrictions between Samaritans and the Jews. She proclaims that Jacob and his sons where greater than Jesus (vs. 12) and that the mountain that they worshipped in was the proper place to do so (vs. 20). Jesus tells her that she does not know what she is talking about. He reveals to her that *"salvation is of the Jews"*. The word "of" in Jesus' statement is very important because it is a statement of origins. The Amplified Bible's translation of this verse

illuminates what Jesus meant when He said
salvation is *"of the Jews"*. Specifically, it says:

> *"You [Samaritans] do not know that you
> are worshipping [you worship what you
> do not comprehend]. We do know what
> we are worshiping [we worship what we
> have knowledge of and understand], for
> [after all] salvation comes from [among]
> the Jews" (John 4:22).*

Jesus was saying that salvation would come from
or out of the Jewish nation – namely through
Himself. In other words, the *means* by which
man will be enabled to have a relationship with
God, will not be found in a mountain or a well,
but from what will come forth out of the Jewish
nation.

Jesus was not giving instruction concerning one's
soul salvation, but clarifying a private
individual's misunderstanding of how, or through
what means, salvation will be made available to
man. The object was, and always is, the
Kingdom. Jesus points this out when He

identifies himself as the Messiah. Specifically, the text says:

> *"The woman said to Him, "I know that Messiah is coming" (who is called Christ)."When He comes, He will tell us all things." Jesus said to her, "I who speak to you am He" (John 4:25-27).*

The Messiah, or Christ, was understood to be a King that the Jewish people expected to come and delivers them from their oppressors and reestablish the Kingdom. Jesus reveals to this woman that He in fact was the long awaited Messiah King. In other words, the King and His kingdom are here!

Luke 19:5-10

Finally in Luke 19, Jesus visits Zacchaeus, a Jewish tax collector, in his home. Apparently Jesus' teachings struck a chord with Zaccheaus because he repents of his past transgressions and declares that He will restore four times over anyone he has defrauded. Jesus responds to Zaccheus' confession and repentance by declaring:

> *"Today salvation has come to this house, because he also is a son of Abraham; "for the Son of Man has come to seek and to save that which was lost "*
> *(Luke 19:9-10).*

The context of this conversation is very important in understanding what Jesus actually meant when He declared that, *"salvation has come to this house"*. Jesus' statement was not an indication that Zaccheaus could buy his salvation by repaying those he had stolen from. It appears that Jesus had provided some teaching prior to Zaccheaus' confession and commitment. We know Jesus primary message was the Kingdom. Jesus in declaring the Kingdom also announced as part of His Gospel message the means by which on enters the Kingdom. Specifically, Jesus declared: *"Repent for the Kingdom of Heaven is at hand"* (Matthew 4:17). Therefore, repentance, or the changing of the way one thinks, is a prerequisite for one qualification to enter God's Kingdom. John the Baptist, like Jesus, preached that repentance was prerequisite for entrance into the Kingdom (Matthew 3:2, 4:17).

Like Nicodemus in John 3, Zaccheaus was a Jew, and anxiously awaited the arrival of the Messiah King and the restoration of the Kingdom. Like Nicodemus, Zaccheaus was also aught that you gained entrance into the Kingdom through: (1) strict adherence to the Law and (2) their being descendant of Abraham. Jesus' news, that neither works nor the flesh qualified you for admission to the Kingdom must have been welcome news for Zaccheaus, especially in light of his occupation and his obvious violation of the Jewish laws against usury and unjust gain. Zaccheaus' sincere repentance, submission to and faith in Christ demonstrated the necessary qualification for entrance to the Kingdom. Again, this isolated, private conversation for the purpose of clarifying one's understanding of how they enter the Kingdom cannot be taken as authorization to establish salvation as the foundation of Jesus' Gospel.

To Seek and Save "That"

Jesus said in Luke 19:10, *"For the Son of man is come to seek and to save **that** which was lost"* *(underline and bold added).* In order to gain a clear understanding of what Jesus meant when speaking about "seeking" to save that which was lost, we can look at previous statements He made concerning what should be the top priority of our seeking.

Specifically, in Matthew's gospel, Jesus commands us to *"seek first the Kingdom of God"* (Matthew 6:33). Jesus being the second Adam, and corporeal representative of all mankind, came seeking and to secure the same thing that all mankind is commanded to seek first – the

Kingdom. Therefore, when Jesus says that He came to *seek* and *save* or *secure "that"* which was lost, it can be inferred that He is referring to the Kingdom.

Secondly, another insight from our scripture that confirms this understanding is the use of the word "that". In Luke 19:10 Jesus points out that He came to secure *"that"* which was lost, not *"they"* or *"them"* who are lost. Specifically, Jesus says that the object that He seeks to secure is not a *"they or them"*, but a *"that"*!

A final insight that Jesus provides to our identifying the object of His pursuit or seeking, is that it is something that *was* lost – past tense. Jesus would not speak of those He came to save in past tense, but in the present. He clearly indicates that the object He sought to secure was a "that" and not "them", and was something that "was" lost, not is lost. People, who are lost, are presently lost. To say that a person *was* lost is an omission that they are no longer lost. Therefore, Jesus' statement can only mean that the object that He is seeking is something that: (1) is not a person or group of people, and (2) *was* lost at some time in the past.

This is important, because if we replace the word *"that"* with *"they"* or *"them"*, we significantly alter Jesus' intent, as well as, our understanding of the message that we are to advance in the earth. Unfortunately, we have consciously or unconsciously, replaced the word *"that"* with *"they"* resulting in our primary message and focus being the salvation of "*them" which are lost*, to the exclusion of the revelation and securing of "*that"* which *was* lost – the Kingdom!

Salvation, the Means to an End

Salvation is the *"means" to an "end"*. The Kingdom is the *object* or the *end*, while *salvation*

56

is the *means* by which it is acquired. In John chapter 3 Jesus is holding a conversation with Nicodemus; who came to Him in the middle of the night. Specifically, the text reads:

> *There was a man of the Pharisees named Nicodemus, a ruler of the Jews. This man came to Jesus by night and said to Him, "Rabbi, we know that You are a teacher come from God; for no one can do these signs that You do unless God is with him." Jesus answered and said to him, "Most assuredly, I say to you, unless one is born again, he cannot see the kingdom of God." Nicodemus said to Him, "How can a man be born when he is old? Can he enter a second time into his mother's womb and be born?" Jesus answered, "Most assuredly, I say to you, unless one is born of water and the Spirit, he cannot enter the kingdom of God" (John 3:1-5).*

Jesus explained to Nicodemus, a religious leader within the religious community, that, the way by which you enter the Kingdom is through a spiritual transaction, not through the works of the flesh. He was using a physical analogy of birth to communicate a spiritual reality to him. Just as physical birth is the entrance or doorway into this physical world, spiritual birth is how we likewise enter into God spiritual Kingdom. Jesus was not establishing a doctrine through this single discourse in the middle of the night to a single individual. He was simple illuminating the means to obtaining the object or end.

Nations of the World

One consequence of the church's emphasis on the salvation gospel to the exclusion of the rest of the gospel is an individualized and institutionalized faith. For many, salvation is an individualist event. It is said, in churches and Christian families, to unsaved family members that we pray for their salvation. After months and even years of praying for an individual, they finally come to confess Jesus as their Lord and Savior, culminating in their conversation being recognize in a church setting. This individual, without further instruction in the rest of the gospel, will come to the conclusion that they have achieved the objective with their soul being saved. However, from the Full Gospel's perspective, they have just begun their journey. Their soul's salvation was not the culmination, but the qualification for the initiation of their manifesting their sonship and the Kingdom in the earth.

In the truest sense the gospel's focus has never been upon individuals but nations of the world. Jesus said:

> *"And this gospel of the kingdom shall be preached in all the world for a witness unto all nations; and then shall the end come" (Matthew 24:14).*

Also,

> *"Go therefore and make disciples of all the nations, baptizing them in the name of the Father and of the Son and of the Holy Spirit" (Matthew 28:19).*

And,

> *"And the gospel must first be preached*
> *to all the nations" (Mark 13:10).*

Jesus intended for the gospel to be more than an individual's personal experience, but a national influence. Like leaven placed within a lump of dough, it gradually transforms the character of its host until the entire lump is impacted by the leavens presence. This is the ultimate objective of our salvation. This is why when God sends his Gospel to us He specifically identifies nations as the object.

It is interesting to note that the word gentile in the Greek does not mean unbeliever, but is the word *"goy"* which means nations. Specifically, in the New Testament we are introduced primarily to 2 gospels for two groups. The first gospel is to the Jews and it is a gospel "concerning Jesus Christ, while the second gospel is to the gentiles and is the "gospel of Christ" or the gospel of the

Kingdom. The first gospel's purpose is to convince the Jew that Jesus' is (was) the Messiah King they were waiting for. The gospel to the gentiles was the Gospel that Jesus proclaimed publically, which was the restoration of God's Kingdom in the earth for all that will enter. The Jews did not need the revelation of the Kingdom, because it was originally delivered to them and they were expecting it return. They did not need to be instructed in the Kingdom, only God's new protocol for entering – faith in His Son Jesus Christ. We will cover this in more detail later in this book.

However, it must be understood that God intentions were that the gospel's focus be upon the nations of the world, not for it to become an individualized, institutionalized internal message that fails to influence the culture it was given to impact and transform. (See Mt 24:14; 28:19; Mark 13:10, Luke 24:47).

FULL GOSPEL

Saved but Stuck

FULL GOSPEL

Saved but Stuck

henever we teach the Gospel, and the means replaces its object, those who receive this gospel inevitably come to a place of paralysis and stagnation. This is due to their having achieved the object of their expectation without receiving further direction on how their salvation translates into their overall purpose. We've all seen it before; where friends and family pray for a loved one who has been holding out on coming to the Lord. Every opportunity we get we remind them that they need to get saved so that they won't have to experience the horrors of hell. After much resistance and trials, they finally come to church and give their life to Christ. The family and church celebrates the individual's salvation. The individual arrives home after much celebration and ado over getting saved. In the individual's eyes, they have completed and achieved what everyone in their family has been telling them for years – *that they must get saved.* After the passing of time and much religious activity (going to church, new member's class, bible study and special activities etc...) they begin to wonder: "What's next?" More than likely they are being attacked by the enemy and trying to *live right.* Meanwhile, in the midst of this warfare, the only solace they are given is that; one of these days God is going to take them away from all of the pain suffering and problems.

If nothing else is imparted to the individual, their hope will dissipate and they will faint in their situation. They come to realize that their souls may have been saved from hell, but they end up experiencing hell on earth. They made it inside the doors of the church through the salvation message, but then become stuck in the church without the revelation of the Kingdom!

This is not God's intention; neither is it the "good news" or the Gospel that Jesus deliver to the church. The ministry and message that Jesus demonstrated for us was one of power and victory. He empowered us to do work in the earth until His return. Our salvation is not a *diploma* but our *admission or acceptance letter!* It is the means by which we become qualified to enjoy the rest of what Jesus has purchased and given us.

The salvation that Jesus delivered to us is more than a message; it contained the fullness, fulfillment and life satisfaction that God provided for man when He gave man His Kingdom to enjoy.

Waiting on Heaven

Those who adhere to the salvation only message often discern a lack of power in their lives. They read the precious promises of God in the Bible and wonder why these things are not manifesting in their lives. They are dealing with the same issues, problems and struggles they had before they were saved. In some instances, things may have even grown worse because of the warfare being waged due to their decision to live according to God's Word and standards. The reason for this is that they've been instructed on how to get saved, but not on how to experience and manifest the benefits of their salvation.

Throughout the gospels, you will notice that whenever the Gospel of the Kingdom was preached there was healing and deliverance from the power and works of the devil (Matthew 4:24, 9:35, 10:8). The hearer of this message was empowered to experience restoration in whatever area of their lives they had a need of being restored. The salvation was not confined to their souls, but extended to impact their bodies and their everyday lives.

The salvation only gospel creates a contradiction in the life of many believers because it promised victory, but postpones the enjoyment of their victory to after they die. Most people, when they come to Christ, are struggling to overcome a situation in their current life situation; and need salvation and deliverance from it in the here and now. To preach a gospel of salvation that does not address their immediate need, causes the newly born and still immature believer to become confused as to the utility of their salvation for the present situation. As a result , those who receive the salvation only realize that they are saved, while at the same time stuck! They receive instruction on the rewards that await them in the "after life" or "life to come", but receives little or no instruction on what to do with the time they have left here in *this life*. They are told that they are to go out and win the lost to Christ, while not truly understanding the purpose for which they are saved. They are saved and left in the earth only to await death. They are saved and left here in the earth to advance God's Kingdom in the earth and to prepare the way for the return of our King. Contrary to popular belief, Christ did not save us to go to heaven, but to stay here in the earth as His ambassadors. If the object of our lives here in the earth was to become born again, or saved, once we accomplished this milestone, there would be no further purpose for us to remain here. This being the case, once we confessed Christ as our Lord and Savior, God would have every right to rapture us into His presence the moment our confession of faith left our lips. This was not God's intention that we leave the earth, but remain her to impact it for the Kingdom of God. Jesus makes this clear when He prays to the Father and says:

""I do not pray that You should take them out of the world, but that You should keep them from the evil one" (John 17:15).

This truth is further seen in the book of Revelation, after God's Kingdom has subdued every other kingdom, we are told that:

"Now I saw a new heaven and a new earth, for the first heaven and the first earth had passed away. Also there was no more sea. Then I, John, saw the holy city, New Jerusalem, coming down out of heaven from God, prepared as a bride adorned for her husband. And I heard a loud voice from heaven saying, "Behold, the tabernacle of God is with men, and He will dwell with them, and they shall be His people. God Himself will be with them and be their God" (Revelations 21:1-3).

Again, verse 10 of this same chapter says:

"And he carried me away in the Spirit to a great and high mountain, and showed me the great city, the holy Jerusalem, descending out of heaven from God."

God's *original* plan is also His *ultimate* plan for man; That man's earthly kingdom be a reflection of God heavenly kingdom. As a matter of fact, this is what Jesus says should be a priority in our prayer life (see Matthew 6:10).

The religious notion of our being transported to some unearthly spiritual abode to spend eternity as is unscriptural. This is why Jesus spent so much time teaching us about how to live life here on earth; because this is where we will spend eternity (Revelation chapter 21).

Dying to Be Blessed

One reason those who adhere to the salvation only gospel become stuck in their walk is because they have assigned all their hope for being blessed and experiencing fulfillment in life *post mortum* – or after they die and *go to heaven*. In other words, they believe that they must physically die first before they are entitled to experience God's blessings. This creates a conflict and a contradiction in the mind of the believer; because it is difficult to understand why God would reserve his blessings for a place (heaven) where we will have no needs? You won't need healing, provision, peace and wholeness in heaven because sickness, lack, distress and division is not present in heaven. These are conditions found in the life of believers here and now. Therefore, it would make no sense to withhold these benefits until one dies. This doctrine is Satan's attempt to cause believers to live beneath their privilege and forsake the restoration Jesus purchased with His blood. As a matter of fact, Satan has convinced many that it is God's will for their life that they endure that which Christ died to deliver them from. This not only diminishes the work of Christ on the cross, but mischaracterizes God and His nature as being something other than good toward man. As mentioned previously, this gospel is no gospel at all; but is a doctrine of demons designed to cause the believer forfeit their enjoyment of the blessings and benefits of their salvation.

The truth of the matter is that Jesus came to give us life and life more abundantly (John 10:10). The Full Gospel of Christ is one of ever increasing life.

Mankind was created for the earth, and the earth was created to be inhabited by man (Isaiah 45:18). God's intention was that spirit filled man would live with God in His earthly Kingdom forever (See Revelations chapter 21). Due to man's fallen condition and the world being filled with sin, God had to progressively restore His will for us in the earth. God progressively implemented measures to prepare the earth and man for the glorious culmination of His plan by giving us: (1) His precious promises, (2) the revelation of His will through His Word, (3) His Law, (4) the manifestation of His Son Jesus in the flesh, (5) His Son's blood as a sacrifice for our sins, (6) gifts and the indwelling of His Holy Spirit, and (6) immediate access by faith and the Holy Spirit to His Kingdom.

All of these blessings and benefits God gave to man while he is yet alive here on earth. God never intended for us to have to die in order to experience what Christ died to give us. The Bible calls what Jesus gave us both *gifts* and an *inheritance*. Both of these provisions are for our benefit while we are alive here on earth.

Benefits and Inheritance

When speaking of our receiving the benefits that are found in the inheritance God has given us, it is not *our* death that is the qualifying event that triggers the release of our inheritance, causing it to become possessory. Legally, the qualifying death is that of the *testator,* not the *beneficiary*.

In other words, the one who makes the promise to bestow their property to identified heirs must die first so that the *"still living"* heirs can take of what has been promised. Dead heirs are not heirs at all! Beneficiaries must be alive to benefit from what has been given them by the testator.

A contemporary example of this principle would be if a father wrote a will wherein he states: *"It is my will and desire that all of my children, by my only wife, receive and share equally in all of my possessions"*

It is assumed that: (1) the father property will not be distributed until he dies, and (2) the children who receive the inheritance are alive at the time of the father's death in order to legally take possession of their father's property.

However, we have religiously turned this around and said to the children must die (go to heaven) first in order to receive what the father has promise them. This makes no sense. The death of the child is not the qualifying event, but the death of the testator. Specifically, the writer of the book of Hebrews addresses this issue in describing the work of Christ toward us when he wrote:

> *"For where there is a testament, there must also of necessity be the death of the testator. For a testament is in force after men are dead, since it has no power at all while the testator lives."* *(Hebrews 9:16-17).*

Jesus, knowing that He must die in order for the promises of God to become our possession promised to give us our inheritance upon his death. This kind of gift is legally referred to as a *"Gift Causa Mortis"*. A *"Gift Causa Mortis"* is a gift of personal property made in contemplation of the donor's imminent death upon the condition that the donor dies as anticipated. Once the donor dies, the property immediately vests in the indentified donee. There is nothing further for the donee to do in order to be a beneficiary of the gift. Specifically, we find in John's Gospel:

> *"Nevertheless I tell you the truth. It is to your advantage that I go away; for if I do not go away, the Helper will not come to you; but if I depart, I will send Him to you.' ... "He will glorify Me, for He will take of what is Mine and declare it to you. "All things that the Father has are Mine. Therefore I said that He will take of Mine and declare it to you" (John 16:7, 14-15).*

We know that the Kingdom of God is where the Holy Spirit resides (Luke 17:20-21 and Romans 14:17). Therefore, these gifts and precious promises are not for our enjoyment after we die, but while we are yet still alive. When Jesus died, His death was the qualifying event which made what He promised possessory to the beneficiaries.

It is interesting to note that the only way a *Gift Causa Motis* does not become possessory is if the *donee* implicitly or expressly refuses to accept the gift. No one else has this power. The donee can act in such a way that they demonstrate their refusal of the gift, thereby forfeiting their enjoyment of it. This is what is happening in the church today based on flawed doctrine. Christ died and gave men gifts, but we are rejecting them because we have been taught that they are not for us in this life, but in the life to come. Therefore, we suffer sickness, lack and insufficiency, not because God has not provided for us, but because we refuse to receive what He has provided to meet our needs. Specifically,

> *"But to each one of us grace was given according to the measure of Christ's gift. Therefore He says: "When He ascended on high, He led captivity captive, and gave gifts to men" (Ephesians 4:7-8).*

These gifts were given by Christ as He ascended to heaven. Those He gave gifts to were not in heaven, but on earth. There are no needs in heaven. Gifts would be of no value in the presence of the Source and Giver of every good and perfect gift. Why would God restrict our enjoyment of such gifts as provision, healing and deliverance; only to be made available to us when we die and go to heaven when none of these needs exist there? This would be like telling a sick man, that he can only receive the cure to his disease once he dies; then we'll administer him the cure. No! These blessings and gifts have been given to us as provision for our lives, here in a world, where there are needs of every kind. You do not have to die to be blessed. Your inheritance was given to you to enjoy right here, right now, in God's Kingdom here on earth.

Milk

"Like newborn babies you should crave (thirst for earnestly desire) the pure (unadulterated) spiritual milk, that by it you may be nurtured and grow unto [completed] salvation."
1Peter 2:2 (AMP)

I can remember when my wife and I had our first child. Our son weighed a bouncing 10 pounds and was always hungry. I remember my wife and I retiring at night for some much needed rest, and my son waking us up every 2 hours to be fed. It was especially hard on my wife because she decide to breast feed him. Therefore, when my son would awake to be fed, my wife would have to rise from the bed, take him in her arms and feed him until he went to sleep. She would fall asleep after feeding him only to be awakened again by his cry wanting more milk to satisfy his seemingly insatiable appetite. Having endured this for a couple of weeks we decided to share the duties by switching him to bottles and formula, so that I could join her in this *fellowship of suffering.*

After a period of time something strange began to happen. He began to sleep for only 30 minutes, instead of the traditional 2 hours, between feedings. He would awake hungry as if he had not recently been fed. This being our first child, we did not know what to do, so we called my wife's mother for advice. Her advice was simple, but profound and spoke to me on several levels. She advised that we add cereal to his milk, to add more substance to his diet, which in turn will cause him to feel full and sleep longer. She explained that the milk was no longer enough to satisfy his bodies growing needs. We took her mother's advice and sure enough, he began to sleep longer . As he grew, we added more and more cereal to his meal until he ultimately transitioned into solid food. We discovered that milk was suitable and necessary for our child's beginning, but it quickly became insufficient as he grew. He now needed something more solid and weighty to sustain his proper development.

The Apostle Peter calls upon this same analogy to demonstrate the purpose of the milk of God's Word has in the growth and development of new believers. Peter says that milk is something you begin on and should out grow. The Amplified translation of the Bible illuminates Peter's statement in 1Peter 2:2 by declaring that milk is designed to facilitate growth onto *"completed salvation"*. In other words, it is intended to grow the believer toward a greater level of understanding and maturity; not simply sustain them in a perpetual state of immaturity. The above plainly states that the salvation event is not the culmination of the believer's experience, but the beginning of a process that leads to a greater revelation of the purpose of their salvation – the Kingdom of God!

Meat

"I fed you with milk and not with solid food; for until now you were not able to receive it, and even now you are still not able" (1Corinthians 3:2).

The Apostle Paul, in writing to the church at Corinth and echoes Peter's sentiment concerning their being a greater dimension of revelation that is available to the believer beyond the salvation event. Paul calls this greater dimension of revelation "solid food" or "meat". He explains that he started the believer out on milk because they were young and could not handle weightier food. However, it is expected that the believer should outgrow the elementary things, and move onto a weightier diet of the Word, resulting in maturity.

One reason why the salvation only messages is so harmful to the Body of Christ is because it causes the believer to become the object instead of the Kingdom. They believe because now that "they're saved" that all is well – mission accomplished. Their salvation was the object of Christ's work and now all of their expectation is focused on making it to heaven. This selfish perspective of the plan of God does not take into consideration that God is depending upon the newly born again believer to mature so that they can advance God's Kingdom throughout the earth. God's plan is not focused on any one individual, but nations of individuals. These individuals, once saved are expected to grow unto maturity, so that they can influence others and advance the Kingdom of God in the areas in which they've been assigned. They are to reproduce believers and influence their territory for the Kingdom. However, only that which is mature can reproduce. That is a law in the Kingdom of God and nature. Nothing that is immature can reproduce. In other words, that which is immature can only take, it cannot give. It is a consumer not a producer. Only that which is mature has the power to reproduce and give. This is why we cannot become stuck on a diet that only provides us with instructions on how to get saved. We must mature so that we can become productive citizens of the Kingdom.

Maturity requires meat. Only meat can provide the substance and strength necessary to empower one with the ability to be reproductive and to wage a successful warfare in taking territory for the Kingdom!

Beyond Foundations

No one digs a foundation for a home without the expectation that something of greater value will be built upon it. The foundation is important, but it is only the first step in manifesting its purpose and object.

The writer of Hebrews, who many believe to be Paul, wrote that believers, after a period of time should move beyond the elemental teachings such: salvation, faith in Christ and turning away from sin, etc.... He says that they should mature and graduate to weightier revelations of God's will for them. Specifically, the write of Hebrews wrote:

"For though by this time you ought to be teachers, you need someone to teach you again the first principles of the oracles of God; and you have come to need milk and not solid food. For everyone who partakes only of milk is unskilled in the word of righteousness, for he is a babe. But solid food belongs to those who are of full age, that is, those who by reason of use have their senses exercised to discern both good and evil" (Hebrews 5:12-14).

Also,

"Therefore, leaving the discussion of the elementary principles of Christ, let us go on to perfection, not laying again the foundation of repentance from dead works and of faith toward God, of the doctrine of baptisms, of laying on of hands, of resurrection of the dead, and of eternal judgment. And this we will do if God permits" (Hebrews 6:1-3).

The Amplified Bible's translation of this text further clarifies the writer's statement by adding:

"If indeed God permits, we will [now] proceed [to advanced teaching]"

The writer says that there are *first principles* or *foundations* that he characterizes as *milk* which is appropriate for those who have just been born again. However, he says that we should leave *"discussion of the elementary principles of Christ"* and *"go on to perfection, not laying again the foundation of repentance from dead works etc...."* It is clear that the writer of Hebrews expected the believer to grow beyond elementary knowledge of salvation through Christ and their separation from sin, but onto things that impact the well being of others.

Peter, Paul and the writer of Hebrews, all recognize the need for the introductory message concerning one's salvation and turning from sin. They all declare that milk is essential in establishing a firm foundation upon which the believer can begin their journey onto maturity. However, they also agree that there is a greater purpose in our being saved than our being sustained by others and our abstaining from sin.

There is a place of perfection and maturity that can only be realized as a result of the believer moving beyond their individual salvation experience and into the corporate experience of God's Kingdom. However, this will only take place when they are presented with the *"Full Gospel"*.

Doctrine of Demons

Doctrine of Demons

atan's primary method of attack against the believer and the church is the utilization of deception. Satan does not want to be exposed or discovered, but rather work in the shadows carrying out his diabolical plan. Contrary to popular belief, Satan does not operate in a wild and objectively evil manner, as portrayed in movies and on television. His mode of operation is premised upon stealth and his activity generally bears the appearance of legitimacy and truth. Paul warns that:

> *"Lest Satan should take advantage of us ... we should not be ignorant of his devices"* (2Corinthians 2:11).

Again, Paul warns believers that:

"Satan himself transforms himself into an angel of light" (2Corinthians 11:14).

Jesus warned us that Satan's deception will be so persuasive that, *if it were possible*, he would deceive the very elect of God (Matthew 24:24). In fact, we saw this happen to the very first man and woman who knew God more intimately than any other human being, besides Christ Himself. God's elect had the ability to rebuke Satan with God's Word, but chose to converse and reason with the father of lies. They received his demonic suggestions which caused their conscious to become contaminated with a false perception of God and His nature. The Bible reveals that Eve was deceived by Satan and gave place to steal what God had given them and to wreck havoc upon mankind (2Cor. 11:3, 1Timothy 2:14).

It must be pointed out that the reason Satan must utilize deception is due to the fact that he does not have the authority or power over God or man to defeat them without their permission or participation. This is because God gave man dominion over all the earth. It must be noted that in any kingdom, the king is sovereign and cannot sued for any cause (outside of violation of the original contract he has between him and his citizens) because he owns everything and has all power within his realm. There is no power to compel him to do anything, outside of his own word. The king must give his consent to be sued, and responds to charges at pleasure, not by compulsion. Mankind, having been given dominion in the earth could not be conquered; therefore Satan had to find a way to get what Adam owned by being granted permission. Satan implicitly admits that this is how he gained authority in the world when he admitted to Jesus, during Christ' temptation in the wilderness;

> "All this authority I will give You, and their glory; for this has been <u>delivered</u> to me, and I give it to whomever I wish" (Luke 4:6) (underline added).

Satan admits that he did not acquire his authority and glory of these kingdoms by *conquest*, but *request*. They were voluntarily handed over to him by Adam.

Now that we understand Satan's primary *mode* of attack, deception and stealth, we must also understand the *focus* of his attacks. Satan's primary targets of attack are: (1) the character and name of God, (2) God's Word, (3) God's people, and (4) God's church and Kingdom.

Satan has found a means by which he can attack all of the above mentioned targets at once. This means or method is found in the form of *"church doctrine"*.

Contaminated Doctrine

Any doctrine that denies, diminishes or obscures the truth concerning God's good nature, promises, purposes and people is a doctrine influenced by demons. As mentioned above, these doctrines will not be readily discernible because the enemy knows that good people will not accept and embrace that which is obviously evil or wrong. Therefore, Satan must cause error to be intellectually acceptable, while maintaining the appearance of truth. However, the fruit of this doctrine reveals its true origin. If a doctrine produces apathy, conflict, division, impotence or self centeredness, and does not produce growth, harmony, life, power and the restoration of God's original plan for man, it is not of God.

Satan has focused his attention on the things of God in order to hinder and hopefully destroy the plan of God in the earth. He revealed his primary mode of operation and focus when he engaged Adam and Eve in the Garden. Satan's first question to man concerned the Word of God. He asked Eve: *"Has God said"?* Specifically, he asks Eve:

"Can it really be that God has said, You shall not eat from every tree of the garden?" (Genesis 3:1, AMP).

His purpose was to contaminate man's perspective of God's goodness and motivations for the restriction he placed upon man's right to the Tree of the Knowledge of Good and Evil.

This cannot be overlooked. The first temptation of man concerned his understanding of God's Word. In other words, he developed a doctrine, using a misinterpretation of God's Word that he intended to impact man's relationship with God. By attacking God's Word, Satan was able to, all at once attack: (1) God's good Name, (2) His nature, (3) the integrity of His Word, (4) God's people and (5) His Kingdom. Having succeeded in his use of deception with the first Adam, he again tries to deceive Jesus, the second Adam, in His temptation in the wilderness. Jesus overcomes Satan with the accurate understanding and employment of God's Word. Specifically, Jesus continually reminded Satan that *"it is written ..."* (Luke 4:4, 8).

Satan, having failed in his prior attempts to deceive Jesus reverts to the perversion of God's Word (just as he did with Eve in Genesis 3:1) by quotes Psalms 91:11-12 out of context, and prefacing his deception with the statement *"it is written ..."*. Jesus knowing not only the *letter of the Word*, but the *Spirit of the Word* as well, defeats Satan by responding with the Word that specifically addressed the enemy's attack.

Powerlessness

The Apostle Paul warns his son Timothy that there will be a time coming where men will not want sound doctrine, but will rather prefer that which is easy and gratifying to their flesh. This gospel will be a powerless gospel which, without the power of God as an authenticator of the message, anything will be received as Gospel. Specifically, Paul says:

> *"The time will come when they will not endure sound doctrine, but according to their own desires, because they have itching ears, they will heap up for themselves teachers; and they will turn their ears away from the truth, and be turned aside to fables" (2 Timothy 4:3-4).*

Paul said that sound doctrine will be replaced with a doctrine devoid of truth. It will deny the very truth that the Bible clearly proclaims. Because this doctrine will be demonically inspired and the product of men's intellect, it will have no power to transform peoples' lives. It will have the appearance of truth, but will be unable to accomplish what only truth can accomplish. Men will develop doctrines that excuse and intellectualize the absence of God's power in their message and lives. They will formalize, through religious ritual and tradition error establishing it as doctrine for their adherents.

These unsound doctrines will be based upon half truths. They will emphasize an element of truth to the exclusion of the rest of it. They will confine God's activity and power to another time and dispensation because they themselves have not experienced it, thereby legitimizing in the eyes of their adherents their lack of power and manifestation in their message and ministry.

The Bible warns that the enemy would attack and contaminate what is taught by introducing doctrine that specifically *denies* the "power of God". Specifically, the Word declares:

> *"In the last days perilous times will come: For men will be lovers of themselves, lovers of money, boasters, proud, blasphemers, disobedient to parents, unthankful, unholy, unloving, unforgiving, slanderers, without self-control, brutal, despisers of good, traitors, headstrong, haughty, lovers of pleasure rather than lovers of God, having a form of godliness but denying its power. And from such people turn away! For of this sort are those who creep into households and make*

captives of gullible women loaded down
with sins, led away by various lusts,
always learning and never able to come
to the knowledge of the truth. (2
Timothy 3:1-7, KJV)

Paul says that an identifying characteristic of
unsound doctrine is: (1) it will claim to have a
relationship with God, (2) it will deny the
corresponding ability that flows from that
relationship, and (3) its teachers will appear to be
very knowledgeable and intelligent, but will
never be able to come to the truth. Stated
another way, these individual's will appear to be
exceptionally knowledgeable and intelligent
leaders in the church but will deny the active
work and power of God delivered to the church
for the advancement of His Kingdom.

To further expose Satan's attack upon the
churches doctrine, Paul warns the church at
Corinth that Satan would attack the *"true*
knowledge of God" through what he describes as
arguments, theories, reasonings and other

intellectual arguments that is contrary to God's true nature. Specifically:

> *"Inasmuch as we refute arguments and theories and reasonings and every proud and lofty thing that sets itself up against the {true] knowledge of God; and we lead everything thought and purpose away captive into the obedience of Christ (the Messiah, the Anointed One)"* *(2Corinthinans 10:3-5, AMP)*

Satan's primary means of attack against God's people has always been to attack the character and goodness of God. He must distort our perception of God and cause Him to become something other than good so that we become separated from Him and susceptible to Satanically inspired substitutes for God's goodness, thereby settling for much less than what God has provided and desires for us.

God's Trying to Teach You Something

This deception is seen and taught today by those who expose that God uses sickness, suffering and poverty to teach His people something. This is contrary to sound doctrine and the good nature of God. God does not need to send calamity or distress upon those seeking to serve Him in order to teach them anything. He sent His Holy Spirit to do this. The *Holy Spirit* is our teacher! The Bible clearly teaches that:

> *"The Holy Spirit, whom the Father will send in My name, He will teach you all things, and bring to your remembrance all things that I said to you" (John 14:26)*

Sickness, disease, suffering, lack and poverty are not the rewards of righteousness, nor the lot of those who serve God; but are a consequence of the curse and sin, both of which Jesus delivered us from through His blood, death and resurrection. Specifically, Deuteronomy 28 describes what the effects of the blessing and

103

curse are in the life of an individual. The ills of sickness, disease, poverty and trouble are ascribed to those who choose not to seek God and His ways. I have not found a single instance in the Bible where God *blessed* someone and their situation grew worse. However, the Bible is replete with examples of sickness, disease, lack, insufficiency, poverty and trouble being the result of the presence of the curse. Any theology or doctrine that imputes this charter and nature upon God is not only unsound, but demonically inspired.

Earning Your Blessing

This kind of doctrine is a vestige of the works mentality that was prevalent during Jesus' ministry, which crept into the church after His ascension. In Paul's writing to the church at Galatia , he confronts this kind of doctrine which refuses to accept the finished work of Christ as having freely delivered to them certain blessings that they previously had to strive to earn in their flesh. They perverted the Word and attempted to diminish Christ work in order to keep the believer in bondage and an adherent to their doctrine. Specifically, Paul states:

> "I marvel that you are turning away so soon from Him who called you in the grace of Christ, to a different gospel, which is not another; but there are some who trouble you and want to pervert the gospel of Christ. But even if we, or an angel from heaven, preach any other gospel to you than what we have preached to you, let him be accursed. As we have said before, so now I say again, if anyone preaches any other gospel to you than what you have received, let him be accursed" (Galatians 1:6-9).

Also,

> "O foolish Galatians! Who has bewitched you that you should not obey the truth, before whose eyes Jesus Christ was clearly portrayed among you as crucified? This only I want to learn from you: Did you receive the Spirit by the works of the law, or by the hearing of faith? Are you so foolish? Having begun in the Spirit, are you now being made

perfect by the flesh? Have you suffered so many things in vain--if indeed it was in vain? Therefore He who supplies the Spirit to you and works miracles among you, does He do it by the works of the law, or by the hearing of faith? -- just as Abraham "believed God, and it was accounted to him for righteousness" (Galatians 3:1-29).

Paul appeals to them that the gospel that is being taught them by these other teachers is not a gospel at all. He says that the power they receive and witness as a result of the Gospel he taught them, and their faith in the finished work of Christ and the Holy Spirit, should have been sufficient to convince them that what was being taught by others was error, and could not produce what they had experienced and freely received through faith. These other teachers taught that through self debasement and humiliation that they were growing in righteousness with God; when in fact God did not want their self debasement, but their hearts.

Any lessons that God wants to teach, we can receive instruction by turning to: (1) His Word, and (2) the ministry of the Holy Spirit.

Remember what has been said already concerning Satan's mode of operation and focus of attack. Satan will use demonically inspired doctrine to slander God's good nature and separate His people from His goodness. God does not want to teach us anything through suffering, sickness, disease, lack, insufficiency, poverty, distress and the like. Jesus bore our pain, sickness and disease for us so that we would not have to (Isaiah 53:5, 1Peter 2:24). He became a curse for us so that we would not have to suffer under the curse and that we might be blessed (Gal 3:13-14). Jesus became poor so that we might be rich (2Cor.8:9). Jesus gave us peace so that we would not have to live in distress (John 14:27). Any doctrine that denies or attempts to invalidate the finished work of Christ, and insists upon the believer's acceptance of that which

Christ destroyed and finished on the cross is not sound doctrine!

God is a God of restoration, especially as it pertains to His people. God wants us to teach us of His goodness. He does not need to use distress and calamity to teach the righteous. He has placed the teacher on the inside of us in the person of His Holy Spirit. He is our teacher!

Kingdom-*less* Gospel

One of the most subtle but damaging attacks of the enemy upon the church's doctrine is the exclusion of the Gospel of the Kingdom from its teachings. This has removed from our teaching the very thing God established to confront and conquer the advancement of Satan's kingdom. One has to wonder how something as important as the Kingdom can fall by the wayside when the Bible declares that the Kingdom:

1. Was God's original gift to man (Gen. 1:26-28)

2. Was the purpose for which Jesus came (Isaiah 9:6-7, John 18:37).

3. Was the Gospel Jesus preached and taught (Mat. 4:17, Luke 4:43)

4. Is what Jesus said should be the focus of our prayers (Mat. 6:9-10).

5. Is what Jesus said should be our primary pursuit in life (Mat. 6:33).

6. Is the Gospel Jesus instructed His disciples to preach and teach (Luke 9:1; 10:9).

7. Is the Gospel Jesus commissioned His disciples to take to the nations as a witness before the end comes (Mat. 14:24)

8. Is the power that destroys Satan's Kingdom (Luke 11:17-20)

9. Is the inheritance God has provided for the believer before the foundation of the world (Mat. 25:34).

10. Was the topic of His post resurrection meeting with church leadership (Acts 1:3).

11. Was the message the church taught and proclaimed in building the early church (Acts 8:12, 19:8, 20:25, 28:23, 31).

12. Is the ultimate destination of the believer (Revelation 21:1-10).

As mentioned previously, the word Kingdom is mentioned over 115 times in the Gospels alone. Jesus Himself spoke of the Kingdom over 100 times in the same Gospels.

With the Kingdom occupying such a prominent position in scripture I do not believe its omission is a coincidence. The enemy will do everything he can to obscure and hide the revelation of the Kingdom from man. The reason for this is that the Kingdom is the only message that has the power to overthrow and displace his kingdom. The Gospel of faith, salvation, miracles, signs and wonders or spiritual gifts have the power to destroy Satan's kingdom.

The Kingdom message possesses the power of God to deliver and retake territory for the Kingdom of God. This is why the enemy fears it. We witness this power in the ministry of Jesus, when He proclaimed the Kingdom message.

Specifically, in Mark Chapter One, Jesus entered a synagogue in Capernaum and begins to teach the people on the Kingdom. While He is teaching, a man possessed with devils reveals their presence in the congregation. It is interesting to note what the Bible contributes as the cause for the exposing and ultimate expulsion of the demon. Specifically the text reads:

> "Now there was a man in their synagogue with an unclean spirit. And he cried out, saying, "Let us alone! What have we to do with You, Jesus of Nazareth? Did You come to destroy us? I know who You are—the Holy One of God!" But Jesus rebuked him, saying,

*"Be quiet, and come out of him!" And
when the unclean spirit had convulsed
him and cried out with a loud voice, he
came out of him. Then they were all
amazed, so that they questioned among
themselves, saying, "What is this?
What new doctrine is this? For with
authority He commands even the
unclean spirits, and they obey Him"
(Mark 1:23-27) (underline added).*

The Bible contributes Jesus' *doctrine* as the
source of the power and authority that exposed
and expelled the demon. This is not an isolated
incident; for the Bible goes on to say that Jesus
went about:

*"Preaching in their synagogues
throughout all Galilee, and casting out
demons" (Mark 1:39).*

The revelation seen here is that the devil is not
afraid of church, nor religion or our traditions. It
appears that these demons regularly attended
their services. It was only when the Kingdom
was preached was the devil's presence made
known. The reason this demon did not feel

threatened sitting under the preaching of the
Scribes and Pharisees was because there is no
power in what they taught. The law condemns
and, if not taught in the right spirit can result in
bondage, instead of freedom. Paul testified to the
when he said:

> *"I was alive once without the law, but*
> *when the commandment came, sin*
> *revived and I died. And the*
> *commandment, which was to bring life, I*
> *found to bring death. For sin, taking*
> *occasion by the commandment, deceived*
> *me, and by it killed me" (Romans 7:9-11).*

Satan does not mind this kind of teaching,
because it facilitates condemnation and a death
consciousness. The Gospel of the Kingdom is the
only message that reclaims territory from the
kingdom of darkness. It is the proclamation of
the *"gospel of the Kingdom"* which triggers the
beginning of the end for Satan and his kingdom
(Mat. 24:14). This is the gospel that Jesus
delivered to the church is a gospel of *power*, and
not just words! Paul confirmed this when he

said: *"For the kingdom of God is not in word but in power"* (1 Corinthians 4:20).

Without the Gospel of the Kingdom, the church lacks the power to advance God's plan in the earth. We can preach salvation only it does not have the power to take territory for the Kingdom. It has the power to populate the Kingdom; however it cannot produce mature and equipped believers who can advance God's Kingdom. The Kingdom is a government, premised on the authority and power of God. The proclamation of the Kingdom message is an exercise of authority. It is a declaration to any and all authorities that God's rule and reign in the earth has returned. It brings the restoration and deliverance that all of mankind is longing for!

"This gospel of the kingdom will be preached in all the world as a witness to all the nations, and then the end will come"
Matthew 24:14

Religious Resistance

Religious Resistance

With the Kingdom being the principle message of the Gospels, as well as being the very message Jesus taught and delivered to the church's leadership; How is it that the Kingdom message has not been taught in the church nor the institutions established for the purpose of equipping the church's leadership for ministry? Men and women endure years of instruction in the various aspects of Biblical interpretation, composition and proclamation, and (in most cases) never receive a single course on the Kingdom of God. Yet and still, the Kingdom is the message Jesus commanded us to take to the world as a witness. How is it that such a central and foundational message of the Bible can almost disappear from the lips of those entrusted with declaring it to the masses? The answer can be gleaned by studying the opposition Jesus faced in proclaiming this same Gospel during His earthly ministry.

By reading the Gospel's account of Jesus' ministry we discover that those who opposed His message most fervently were the religious leaders; specifically the Pharisees and Sadducees. Jesus had no problem engaging sinners and gentiles with His message, although they were not the immediate target of His ministry (see Mat. 15:21-28). However, when He did minister to them they were very receptive to His message and often received healing and deliverance by placing their trust (faith) in Him. As a matter of fact, there is only two occasions in the Gospels where Jesus declares that someone has *"great faith"*. Neither one of these individuals were part of the religious establishment, nor were they for that fact even Jewish; but were *gentiles* - the Roman Centurion of Luke 7:9 and the Canaanite woman of Matthew 15:28. Jesus' primary opposition came from those who were responsible for teaching God's people the Word.

The religious establishment resisted Jesus message because it threatened their security and challenged their understanding of God. They were stuck in what God had done, and could not move into what God was doing. They were inflexible and unable to let go of the traditions given them down through the generations, which also maintained their position and privilege within the community. John in his Gospel records the Scribes and Pharisees plainly stating that this was their concern with Jesus and His message when they stated:

"If we let Him alone like this,
everyone will believe in Him, and the
Romans will come and take away both
our place and nation" (John 11:48).

They were not interested in the welfare of the people; regardless of whether or not Jesus' message was delivering, healing and setting people free from Satan's oppression. Their motivations were that of self preservation and prominence.

The Gospel of the Kingdom that Jesus brought threatened their security and challenged them to go beyond the letter of the law and to come into contact with the heart of God. This message declared that the common man now had access to God again and the ability to know Him as he did before the fall. This necessarily threatened the religious leader's position as intermediaries between God and man; and would necessarily require them to acknowledge that God was establishing a new order of priest (1Peter 2:9).

This signaled a transition that they were not willing to take place without a fight – even if they were fighting against God!

"New Doctrine"

The religious establishment's resistance to Jesus' message was primarily based upon jealousy concerning the impact His message had upon the people. It presented them with a peculiar problem because Jesus' message was inherently powerful and they could not deny its legitimacy or produce the kind of manifestation that accompanied His message. Their message was one of words without power; while Jesus' message was of words *confirmed* by power!

Jesus' message was inherently powerful because it was not a religious message but one which announced the presence of God's authority and reign in the earth. When the gospel of the

Kingdom was proclaimed it was an exercise of authority designed to deliver and restore man back to his original condition and position God established for him in His Kingdom in the Garden.

In Mark's gospel we find Jesus entering into the synagogue at Capernaum and teaching the people on the Kingdom. The people upon hearing Jesus' message was astounded by this *doctrine* and by the authority He demonstrated through His message. Specifically, the text says:

> *"And they were astonished at His teaching, for He taught them as one having authority, and not as the scribes"*
> *(Mark 1:21-22).*

The text goes on to say:

> *"Then they were all amazed, so that they questioned among themselves, saying, "What is this? What new doctrine is this? For with authority He commands even the unclean spirits, and they obey Him" (Mark 1:27).*

The people immediately compared Jesus' message with that of the Scribes and declare that Jesus' message had authority, *not as the scribes*. This immediately placed Jesus at odds with the religious establishment's leadership because the Scribes were seen as the *authority*, as it pertained to the Word of God.

The text goes on to reveal that not only were the people impacted by Jesus' message, but demonic spirits and strongholds that had become entrenched within the synagogue. The declaration of the Kingdom in this synagogue caused territory, which was once under the influence of the kingdom of darkness, to be threatened by a greater authority - the Kingdom of God. This declaration of the Kingdom upset the authority structure in the synagogue so much so that a demonic presence cried out and begged to be let alone (Mark 1:24).

The people described this combination of word and authority as a *"new doctrine"*. In reality, this was not anything new, but the restoration of man as God's spirit filled representative in the earth empowered to fulfill his assignment; that is to *have dominion*! (Gen 1:26, 28).

As we discovered earlier in this book; Satan is very interested in the church's doctrine and religious matters. Satan seeks to influence those who are in leadership to promulgate a doctrine that denies and obscures the true knowledge of God and His Gospel to the people. The religious resistance Jesus and the early church experienced as a result of proclaiming the Gospel of the Kingdom was a result of satanic influence. Jesus recognized this and declared that their father or source was the devil (John 8:44).

The Kingdom message is a message that exercises influence over territory, threatening structures and institutions that have been used

123

by Satan to bind God's people, instead of liberating them. Even after Jesus' death and ascension His message retained its power to heal, deliver and set free those suffering from sickness, infirmity, oppression and lack.

This Gospel of the Kingdom is not just another doctrine, but a *provision* given men from God to restore His order in the earth. This is why Satan fights so vehemently against it being taught and proclaimed to God's people; for it bears the power to overthrow and undo His kingdom!

Bound Again

If we were to dissect the word "religion" we would discover that why this is the case. The word religion is comprised of the prefix "re" and the word "ligion or "ligare". The prefix *"re"* means *"to do again"*, *"do over"* or *"to return to a previous state of being"*. This prefix has dramatic impact upon our theology, for it prefaces such important words such as: rebirth, reconciliation, repentance, restoration, redemption, revelation etc... All of these words are pointing the reader to a former state of being, or the process of doing over or again. The second word is *"ligion"* which comes from the Latin word *"ligio"* or *"ligare"*. *The word "ligare"* means to: *be held together by a band, to bind or restrain.* If we were to combine these two words we would come to understand that religion, for all intensive purposes is to: *"cause one to become bound again".*

If we were to study the New Testament, and specifically the Gospels, we will discover that Satan uses religious people and the establishment to attack and obstruct the advancement of the gospel and God's Kingdom. This is why Satan and his demons are not intimidated by religion and are comfortable in religious settings. This is because, often the objective and outcome of religious activity is the same as their objectives – bondage.

Jesus came to set the captives free. Those who the Son sets free are free indeed. The Son came proclaiming free access to the Kingdom. Those in the religious establishment during Jesus' ministry did everything they could to keep the people from receiving the message of the Kingdom.

Liberty cannot be found in religion; neither can God be found through religion because God did not create it. Religion is a consequence of the fall and man's attempt to regain what he lost in his relationship with God. God gave man access to Him through a *relationship* not a *religion*. Religion creates *servants*, while relationship creates sons. In religion you must earn your right to have a relationship, while in the Kingdom you are born into that relationship. Servants earn their living, while sons receive it.

These differences in these two institutions
(religion and the Kingdom) illustrate the
impossibility of religion achieving and providing
that which only the Kingdom can provide. This
is why Jesus' message sets people free, while the
religious establishment's message bound people.

Religion is man's attempt to establish a
relationship with God through his effort. Its
origin is earthly; while its object heavenly. The
Kingdom's origin is from heaven, and its object is
to impact the earth. This is why our attempt to
enter into relationship with God cannot be based
upon religion, because its origin did not come
from God. It can only be found through the King
and His Kingdom.

"Of No Effect ..."

Two of the greatest obstacles for believers to
overcome in embracing the Full Gospel are: (1)
unsound doctrine, and (2) *religious tradition*.

The obstacles of unsound doctrine and tradition must be removed from the body of Christ because they cause division (Romans 16:17) and God's Word to be of *no effect* (Colossians 2:8 and Mark 7:7-13). Specifically, the Amplified Bible renders Mark 7:13 as:

> *'Thus you are nullifying and making void and of no effect [the authority of] the Word of God through your tradition, which you [in turn] hand on"*

Man's tradition causes division and cancels out the authority God Word by occupying the place in the believer's life that the Word should occupy. As a matter of fact, it becomes a substitute for the Word of God. How can this be? How can anything nullify or take the place of God's Word? The answer is found in the fact that people place their *faith* in the tradition and not God's Word, depriving the Word of the opportunity to fulfill its purpose in their lives. It is of no effect. The tradition becomes the determining factor as to whether they will or will not do a thing.

The Apostle Paul was well aware of the power and potential of religious traditions, rituals and doctrine to subvert and even become a substitute for God's Word in the life of the believer. This is why he wrote to the church at Corinth:

> *"For Christ did not send me to baptize, but to preach the gospel, not with wisdom of words, lest the cross of Christ should be made of no effect" (1 Corinthians 1:17).*

Paul recognized that tradition and man's intellect or wisdom can oppose the Word until they have more influence upon man's life than the Word does. Peter echoes Paul's sentiment when he wrote:

> *"Knowing that you were not redeemed with corruptible things, like silver or gold, from your aimless conduct received by tradition from your fathers" (1 Peter 1:18)*

Paul and Peter both recognized that the enemy can use baptism, food, drink, holy days and other religious activity to preoccupy people until their focus becomes the external compliance to their traditions instead of trusting in God and His Word.

Remember, we previously defined and qualified the soundness of a doctrine by whether or not it embraces, in its totality: (1) the finished work of Jesus on the cross and His resurrection, (2) the deliverance and restoration of man to God's original condition and position, (3) God's goodness. Any doctrine that ascribes to God as the cause of any work that Jesus died to deliver man from is unsound. Doctrine that has traditionally been taught that God teaches the righteous through suffering, poverty, sickness and the like is unsound. The Holy Spirit and the Word of God is what God has given us as instructors, as well as the 5 fold ministry gifts of the ministry. Specifically:

> *"But the Helper, the Holy Spirit, whom the Father will send in My name, He will teach you all things, and bring to your remembrance all things that I said to you" (John 14:26).*

Also,

> *"He Himself gave some to be apostles,*
> *some prophets, some evangelists, and*
> *some pastors and teachers, for the*
> *equipping of the saints for the work of*
> *ministry, for the edifying of the body of*
> *Christ, till we all come to the unity of the*
> *faith and of the knowledge of the Son of*
> *God, to a perfect man, to the measure of*
> *the stature of the fullness of Christ"*
> *(Ephesians 4:11-13)*

God teaches us through the gifts He has given us:
(1) His Word, (2) His Son Jesus, (3) His Spirit,
and (4) His ministry gift: apostle, prophets,
evangelists, pastors and teachers; not sickness,
suffering and lack. The Bible testifies that God
has used sickness, plagues, famine, lack and the
like to chastise the rebellious and wicked, not the
righteous. We've all heard it said before, from
the pulpit to the pew when someone is sick or
suffering: "Endure it and learn what it is God is
trying to teach you through this". This may
sound religious, but it is not biblical, as it applies
to a child of God who is standing in the

131

righteousness of Christ. This kind of doctrine perverts the believer's perspective of God and mischaracterizes Him as being the cause of that which is a consequence of the curse and fall of man; both of which were a product of man's will - not God's.

I believe this kind of characterization of God is a remnant of Israel's and the churches exposure to pagan religious that believe that they must appease their deity in order to earn its favor. Throughout the Bible we witness self mutilation, human sacrifice and other forms suffering in order to gain the favor of a god.

Jesus died and bore our pain and sickness. The prophet Isaiah was emphatic in his declaration that the Christ would bear these things for us, when he said:

> *"Surely He has borne our griefs and carried our sorrows; Yet we esteemed Him stricken, Smitten by God, and afflicted. But He was wounded for our*

transgressions, He was bruised for our iniquities; The chastisement for our peace was upon Him, And by His stripes we are healed" (Isaiah 53:4-5)

The Amplified Bible translates the word *griefs* as: sickness, weaknesses, and distresses. Isaiah says that Christ has *"surely"* accomplished this for us. If Christ died to accomplish this, why would we assume that we must bear them, thereby causing what He purchased for us to be of no effect in our lives?

Gate Keepers

I truly believe that the Full Gospel of the Kingdom is what all mankind, not only believers, are seeking! Whenever I talk or teach about the Kingdom I notice that people are very interested in the Kingdom and always want to know how they can learn more. This is because it is not a religious message. It is a message about man's restoration and God's provision to accomplish this.

With this being the case, it must be asked: *"Why are our churches not teaching the people on the Kingdom?"* The answer cannot be found by looking to the pews, but the pulpit.

I believe a major reason for this omission is that the Full Gospel of the Kingdom is not being preached because it was never being preached or taught to those who are leaders in the church. You can only give what you've received. As mentioned earlier in this writing, our church leaders are graduating from Bible colleges, universities and seminaries that do not offer a single course of study on the Kingdom. Therefore, they are not equipped to instruct their membership in that which they have not been instructed in themselves.

A second reason I believe the Kingdom message has not been proclaimed is due to a more diabolical reason. In the first instance, the church's leadership was in a sense, the victim of not having been instructed in the Kingdom by those who were responsible for instructing them.

However, in the second case, the leaders themselves have intentionally decided to obscure the revelation of the Kingdom from the people. The Bible says in Matthew 23:13 that there are individuals who have positioned themselves at the gates of the Kingdom to keep those who would enter in from entering. Specifically, the Bible says:

> *"But woe to you, scribes and Pharisees, hypocrites! For you shut up the kingdom of heaven against men; for you neither go in yourselves, nor do you allow those who are entering to go in."*

These *"gate keepers"* are men and women who objectively possess the credentials of leadership, but lack a true relationship with God. Their relationship with the Word is not a personal or intimate one, but based upon intellect and their familiarity with scripture and the mechanics of *Christianity* and *church life*. They've never personally had an experience with the power of God in their lives or ministries; therefore, they quickly dismiss any message that declares that God's power is available in our everyday lives. They resist the prospect that God still performs miracles, and challenge the notation that the Gospel is more than a doctrine. They fight to keep the gospel an intellectual matter because they can use their trained intellects to fashion arguments and doctrines that institutionalize impotence as normal; thereby explaining away their inability to demonstrate the power of God in their lives. An intellectualized gospel enables those who are in control to monitor and determine who can enter into the church, specifically into church leadership. I must say that I do not believe that there should be no censorship or qualification of those who teach in or lead in the body of Christ. There definitely needs to be a level of scrutiny and qualification for those who declare that they are called by God to assume any position of leadership in the church. However, when those who are responsible for verifying God's calling upon an individual life, do not have a relationship with God themselves and have other motivations for their decisions, other than ensuring the authenticity of one's message and calling these individuals become barriers to God's plan, rather than protectors of it. They are more concerned with protecting their positions and maintaining control than declaring the truth.

 If they themselves have not personally laid their hands upon you, or given their approval of your ministry, then you are deemed illegitimate and they will do what they can to destroy your creditability. The enemy thrives in this kind of environment, because it is devoid of the leading of the Holy Spirit and can facilitate just about any doctrine or vise that can be produced by human reason.

This was one reason the Pharisees and Sadducees fought so hard against Jesus and His message; He was not one of them, nor had they had anything to do with the development of His message. Jesus did not fit into their institution. Because He did not submit to them, or their doctrinal and religious strictures, He could not be permitted to teach "their people". Anyone found to have gone to one of Jesus' meetings, or professed faith in Him, was excommunicated from the fellowship of their synagogues.

The *gate keepers* of Jesus' day tried to discredit Him, but could not do so because: (1) He not only knew the letter of the law, but the Spirit upon which the letter was given, (2) the miracles He performed confirmed His words, and (3) they could not reproduce His message's results.

To allow the people to enter into the Kingdom and experience the power of God, which is absent in their own lives and messages, would spell the end of the "kingdom" they've been maintaining. Therefore, they must obscure the revelation of the Kingdom, and fortify their position by binding the people with religion, doctrine and traditions, which causes the Gospel of Christ to be of no effect (See Romans 1:16 and Mark 7:13).

These gate keepers have institutional and intellectualize impotence within the Church stripping it and the believer of the power to fulfill their mandate – to have dominion! They have dispensationally confined every objective manifestation or ability given to the church by God to advance His Kingdom.

Despite the fact that these "gate keepers" have, to a degree, succeeded in excluding the Kingdom message from our bible schools, seminaries and churches; God in these last days has sent for the revelation of His Kingdom to His people. The people have begun to demand more than just a nice message, but the manifestation of God's power in their lives. He is taking those who, from all objective standards, do no qualify to proclaim the Gospel and using them to restore the foundations upon which the church and the Kingdom of God were established. They were not built on the doctrine or wisdom of men, but the power of God!

> *"And my speech and my preaching were*
> *not with persuasive words of human*
> *wisdom, but in demonstration of the*
> *Spirit and of power"*
> *1 Corinthians 2:4*

The FULL Gospel!

The FULL Gospel!

The best way for us to determine what is the *Full Gospel*, and what is not, is not by looking around at what is being preached or taught today, nor by asking any of our contemporaries their opinions, but by turning to scripture and examining what Jesus taught and delivered to the church as the Gospel. By studying Jesus' message, and those He discipled, we can gain insight into what was, and was not, considered the Gospel.

It is evident from the condition of the Body of Christ today that something is missing in what we are declaring as the Gospel. Although we claim to have the answer to the world's woes, statistically we fair no better than the world in our health, finances, marriages and morality. I believe this is in a large part due to our over emphasis of one aspect of the Gospel, to the exclusion of the rest of it. In other words, we are not proclaiming a *Full Gospel*. We have placed an inordinate amount our focus on getting the individual to the introductory salvation experience, but have failed to provide sufficient insight into *"that"* which they have been saved. As I have stated throughout this book, there are several reasons for this disparity, both natural and supernatural. However, the task still remains to restore to the church the provision God gave man to overcome in life and advance His Kingdom against the kingdom of darkness. Only the Full Gospel, as delivered by Christ can accomplish this. Anything less does not qualify as good news or "The Gospel".

The Full Gospel

I found it interesting, in my search to gain as many definition of what commentators and biblical scholars defined as the Gospel, that I found the most accurate definition coming from a secular source. The Merriam Webster online dictionary defines the word "gospel" is: *(often capitalized) the message concerning Christ, the kingdom of God, and salvation.* WOW! Somehow, the world recognizes that "The Gospel" is not complete unless it provides insight and instruction concerning: (1) Christ, (2) the Kingdom of God, and (3) salvation.

The Amplified Bible recognizes that what the original church shared as the Gospel was not confined or defined to the message of salvation, but also included the revelation of "Jesus as the Messiah Christ" and the "Kingdom of God". Specifically, the Amplified Bible translates, in the book of Acts, phrase *"the word of God"* as

144

meaning: *"concerning the attainment through Christ of eternal salvation in the Kingdom of God"[1].* Just as Merriam Webster's dictionary included in its definition of the Gospel: (1) Christ, (2) the Kingdom of God and (3) salvation; the Amplified Bible likewise recognized that the *"word of God"* or Gospel that was preached in the early church contained the same elements consisting of the revelation of: (1) Jesus as the Christ, (2) the Kingdom of God and (3) salvation.

These extra-biblical resources confirm that the original church understood that the Gospel message was not one dimensional, nor confined to the salvation message alone, but included the complete redemptive and restorative plan of God for mankind. It was inclusive of the Person, ministry and work of Jesus as the Messiah Christ, the necessity of salvation from the consequence of sin, the fall and curse and the

[1] Referencing Joseph Thayer, A Greek-English Lexicon of the New Testament.

reality and return of God's Kingdom in the earth! This was the Full Gospel the early church used to turn the known world *upside down!* (Acts 17:6). Likewise, the church today will again need to embrace and reclaim the Full Gospel in order for it to impact the world and advance God's Kingdom to all nations!

Gospel for the Nations

Throughout the books of Acts, which chronicles the development and growth of the early church, we witness the above mentioned 3 revelations as constituting its Gospel: The Kingdom of God, Jesus as the Christ Messiah, and the message of salvation. Whether or not it was necessary to communicate all 3 revelations or just a specific revelation was dependent upon the audience the speaker was addressing. This was done because Jews required conviction of a different revelation than that of the gentiles.

Ultimately, the Full Gospel was sent, not to the Jews, individuals or group of individuals, but to the nations of the world at large.

To understand this we must overcome our prejudice that Gospel is focused on individuals, when in reality the Gospel is focused on nations. This religious prejudice is an outgrowth of our preoccupation with the message of salvation. As mentioned previously, all of our efforts have been focused on getting the individual to the salvation event. Once the individual becomes saved, they perceive that the object has been achieved (their soul's salvation) and therefore do not pursue the greater object of advancing and reclaiming territory for the Kingdom of God. Therefore, the individual's salvation, and not the transformation of the nations, becomes the focus.

If we were to study God's interaction with individuals in the Bible, we would discover that these individuals were representatives of nations.

God's interaction and covenant with men such as Adam, Noah, Abraham, Moses, David, Solomon and Jesus were all for the purpose of impacting nations. Each individual represented a dispensation of God's grace and dealings with man in preparation for the restoration and revelation of His Kingdom *again* in the earth. This is why Jesus, when speaking of the Gospel to His disciples, repeatedly emphasized that their focus was the nations of the world. Specifically, we find:

> *"And this gospel of the kingdom will be preached in all the world as a witness to all the <u>nations</u>, and then the end will come" (Matthew 24:14).*

> *"Go therefore and make disciples of all the <u>nations</u>, baptizing them in the name of the Father and of the Son and of the Holy Spirit" (Matthew 28:19)*

> *"And the gospel must first be preached to all the <u>nations</u>" (Mark 13:10).*

"And that repentance and remission of sins should be preached in His name to all nations, beginning at Jerusalem" (Luke 24:47).

"And one of them, Caiaphas, being high priest that year, said to them, "You know nothing at all, "nor do you consider that it is expedient for us that one man should die for the people, and not that the whole nation should perish." Now this he did not say on his own authority; but being high priest that year he prophesied that Jesus would die for the nation" (John 11:49-51)

"And the Scripture, foreseeing that God would justify the Gentiles by faith, preached the gospel to Abraham beforehand, saying, "In you all the nations shall be blessed" (Galatians 3:8).

These scriptures testify that Jesus' death and the gospel were all given to impact the nations! This is the reason why the church's influence and impact in society has been diminishing; we have taught a message focused on the individual's salvation experience and not the transformation of the nations in which these individuals live.

This has resulted in the acceptance of such fictions as "separation of church and state", and the belief that our faith is a personal matter. These are deceptions promulgated by the enemy to cause the church to become weak and our Gospel impotent to transform neither the believer's life nor the nations of the world!

The Jewish Nation

Generally speaking, the Gospel presented to the Jews had as its purpose to convince the Jew that Jesus was in fact the Messiah Christ they were expecting. The good news of the Kingdom was implicit in this Messianic message because they understood the Messiah to be the conquering King who would restore the Kingdom unto them. This is clearly seen in Acts 1:6, when Jesus appeared to those who were assembled together

in Jerusalem after His resurrection, when they
asked Him:

> *"Lord, will You at this time restore the
> kingdom to Israel?" (See Mark 15:43).*

Therefore, the Jews did not need instruction in
the revelation of the Kingdom because they were
already expecting the Kingdom's return. By their
acceptance and conviction of Jesus as the
Messiah, they implicitly acknowledge that the
Kingdom has come.

The Jew needed the revelation of Jesus as the
Christ, the long awaited Messiah. This is why the
message preached to the Jews in the New
Testament concerned the *identity* of Jesus as
Christ the Messiah. Specifically, we read:

> *"When Silas and Timothy had come from
> Macedonia, Paul was compelled by the
> Spirit, and testified to the Jews that Jesus
> is the Christ" (Acts 18:5).*

Also,
> *"For with great power he (Apollos) refuted
> the Jews in public [discussions], showing*

*and proving by the Scriptures that Jesus
is the Christ (the Messiah)" (Acts 18:28,
AMP).*

The Gospel to the Jews often entailed the
speaker providing proof of Jesus' identity by
turning to the Old Testament, the Law and the
Prophets to verify and legitimize their message to
them (See Acts chapter 3; chapter 13; and
chapter 28;31). Jesus Himself, when speaking to
a Jewish audience, also utilized the Law and
Prophet to show that they in fact testify of Him
being the Messiah. Specifically, the Bible
records, as Jesus travelled with the two men on
the Emmas Road, that He:

> *"Beginning at Moses and all the
> Prophets, He expounded to them in all
> the Scriptures the things concerning
> Himself"* (Luke 24:27).

Gentile Nations

This kind of discourse was not used when
proclaiming the Gospel to the Gentile because

they did not hold the Jewish law or the declarations made by their prophets as being authoritative or applicable to them. The gentiles, having no prior conviction of God's Word or reliance upon the Law and the prophets needed a different message to bring them to a place of conviction and faith. The gentiles had to be convinced of the One and only true God's desire to enter into relationship with them and extend admission into His everlasting Kingdom by their faith in His Son and King Jesus the Christ. Gentiles understood the important of being a citizen of a peculiar nation, especially if it a powerful one. We witness the high regard that gentiles placed on their national identity, specifically their citizenship within a kingdom, especially if the kingdom is a powerful and prominent one. We see the importance and influence that being part of a powerful kingdom had on the gentile mind illustrated when Paul was twice arrested and announced that he was a

citizen of the Roman Empire. Specifically, in Acts
chapter 16, the text reads:

> *"But Paul said to them, "They have
> beaten us openly, uncondemned
> Romans, and have thrown us into
> prison. And now do they put us out
> secretly? No indeed! Let them come
> themselves and get us out." And the
> officers told these words to the
> magistrates, and they were afraid when
> they heard that they were Romans"
> (Acts 16:37-38).*

Also, in Acts 22, we find that citizenship in a
powerful kingdom was so important that people
were willing to pay large sums of money to
acquire citizenship in that kingdom. Specifically,
the text reads:

> *"And as they bound him with thongs,
> Paul said to the centurion who stood by,
> "Is it lawful for you to scourge a man
> who is a Roman, and uncondemned?"
> When the centurion heard that, he went
> and told the commander, saying, "Take
> care what you do, for this man is a
> Roman." Then the commander came and
> said to him, "Tell me, are you a Roman?"
> He said, "Yes." The commander*

answered, "With a large sum I obtained
this citizenship." And Paul said, "But I
was born a citizen." Then immediately
those who were about to examine him
withdrew from him; and the commander
was also afraid after he found out that
he was a Roman, and because he had
bound him" (Acts 22:25-29).

The Roman Commander desired to be a citizen of Rome so bad that he paid a large sum of money for his citizenship in the Roman Empire. It is estimated that the cost of purchasing citizenship into the Roman Empire was the equivalent of $200,000 to $600,000. *Wow!* Citizenship in a mighty kingdom was esteemed by many to be worth more than a *half a million dollars!*

The concept of transferring once citizenship to a greater kingdom was not a foreign concept to the gentile mind. It would be particularly attractive to them based on the fact that the cost of their citizenship into the Kingdom of God had already been paid for by the blood of Jesus. This is why

Paul used the analogy of moving from one kingdom to another when he wrote to the gentile church at Colossae. Specifically, he wrote:

> *"For he has rescued us from the dominion of darkness and brought us into the kingdom of the Son"* *(Colossians 1:13, NIV).*

Therefore, a message purporting to offer admittance into an everlasting Kingdom, of the King of Kings, would be very interesting.

As part of the Gospel delivered to the Gentiles, they were educated on the power, resurrection, identity and work of Jesus which made their admittance into the Kingdom possible. However, the message's focus was not the identity of Jesus as the Messiah Christ, as it was with the Jewish audience, but the availability of the Kingdom *through,* or *by,* Jesus (1Cor. 1;4, 2Cor. 1:5; 3:4; Gal. 4:7, Eph. 3:21, Php 4:7, 13, 19; 1Pet. 5:10). Therefore, when we witness the Gospel being presented to a gentile audience, we generally find them being *first* receiving the revelation of the Kingdom (or the *object)*, then on the revelation of the *means* by which they have been granted access to the Kingdom – Jesus the Christ.

We see this fact demonstrated in the Book of Acts by Philip and the apostle Paul as they engaged gentile audience with the Gospel. Specifically, we read:

> *"But when they believed Philip as he preached the things concerning the <u>kingdom of God</u> and the name of <u>Jesus Christ,</u> both men and women were baptized" (Acts 8:12).*

> *"So when they had appointed him a day, many came to him at his lodging, to whom he explained and solemnly testified of the <u>kingdom of God</u>, persuading them concerning <u>Jesus</u> from both the Law of Moses and the Prophets, from morning till evening" (Acts 28:23).*

> *"Preaching the <u>kingdom of God</u> and teaching the things which concern the <u>Lord Jesus Christ</u> with all confidence, no one forbidding him" (Acts 28:31).*

For the gentile, the Gospel consisted of both the revelation of the Kingdom *and* of Jesus Christ. Without the gentile having a understanding of the Kingdom *and* Jesus, the Gospel message would be incomplete.

More Accurately

I believe this is what Aquila and his wife Priscilla discerned as they listen to Apollos proclaim the Gospel. Aquilla and Priscilla, after listening to Apollos' gospel perceived that what he was teaching was not incorrect, but definitely incomplete for the audience before him. It must be noted that Apollos was teaching in a gentile city - Ephesus. Specifically, the Bible records:

> *"Now a certain Jew named Apollos, born at Alexandria, an eloquent man and mighty in the Scriptures, came to Ephesus. This man had been instructed in the way of the Lord; and being fervent in spirit, he spoke and taught accurately the things of the Lord, though he knew only*

the baptism of John. So he began to speak
boldly in the synagogue. When Aquila and
Priscilla heard him, they took him aside
and explained to him the way of God more
accurately" (Acts 18:24-26).

The Bible says that after Aquila and Priscilla
listened to Apollos preach, they pulled him aside
and instructed him in the *"way of God more*
accurately". The Bible says that Apollos was: (1)
mighty or well versed in the scriptures, (2)
instructed in the way of the Lord, and (3) knew
only the baptism of John. In other words,
Apollos, being a Jew, had a firm understanding
of: (1) the Law and Prophets, (2) Jesus as the
long awaited Messiah, and (3) John's baptism of
repentance, but failed to also articulate to his
gentile audience the revelation of the Kingdom.

From what we have discovered concerning the
composition of the Full Gospel, the only element
that was missing in Apollos' message was the
Kingdom! I believe that they pulled him aside

and showed him how, from the Scriptures, John's baptism, salvation and Jesus all pointed to the revelation of the Kingdom; and that without the the Kingdom his message was incomplete since both John and Jesus preached the Kingdom (Matthew 3:2, 4:17).

They not only needed instruction in the identity and necessity of faith in Jesus as the Christ and the Savior of their souls, but they also needed instruction in the object and purpose of their salvation - the Kingdom of God.

With the remainder of this chapter, I would like to take a closer look at the message that some of the leading personalities in the New Testament and what they taught as the Gospel. I believe that by taking this look at what they actually taught as the Gospel, we can gain an understanding of the Gospel that we likewise are to take to the nations!

John's Gospel

"The law and the prophets were until John. Since that time the kingdom of God has been preached"

Jesus declares that before John's arrival, the message being taught by the religious establishment consisted of the *"law and the prophets"*. This message consisted of the Law given by Moses and the authoritative and inspired declarations of the nation's prophets. These two sources of instruction formed the foundation and substance of the message presented by the Scribes and Pharisees.

However, when John arrived, he had a different message. He came preaching not law or the prophets, but the arrival of the Kingdom! Specifically, he proclaimed: *"Repent ye: for the kingdom of heaven is at hand"* (Matthew 3:2). The word *"repent"* means more than having remorse or a change in one's conduct. It

161

specifically refers to a change in the way one thinks. The Greek word translated *"repent"* is *"mentanoeo"*. It literally means *"to think differently"*. John, as the forerunner of Jesus, was given the task of initiating a transition in the thinking of God's people. He was responsible for transitioning the people's minds from thinking religiously, to thinking as *royalty*. John had to convince a nation, who believed they had a right to the Kingdom based upon Abraham being their father, that their thinking was wrong. John exposed this error in their thinking when he rebuked them and warned:

> *"Think not to say within yourselves,*
> *We have Abraham to our father: for*
> *I say unto you, that God is able of*
> *these stones to raise up children*
> *unto Abraham" (Matthew 3:9).*

They refused to receive John's gospel, that access to the Kingdom was based on repentance and faith in the Christ, and demanded entrance based on their strict adherence to the law and

Abraham being their forefather. This is what
Jesus meant when He said:

> "Until John came, there were the Law
> and the Prophets; since then the good
> news (the Gospel of the kingdom of God
> is being preached, and everyone strives
> violently to go in [would force his own
> way rather than God's way into it]"
> (Luke 16:16, AMP).

Jesus says that men will demand admittance into
the Kingdom based upon *their* own standard of
righteousness, and not by God's authorized
means. John's Gospel was focused on the
revelation of the Kingdom's presence and
availability to man through the transformation of
man's thinking. God was reestablishing the
order and institution by which men would enter
into relationship with Him. No longer would God
engage men through type and shadows but by
and through His Spirit. Man's relationship was
no longer based on his works as a *servant*, but as
Spirit filled sons through faith in our Lord and
Savior Jesus Christ (Romans 8:14).

Jesus' Gospel

It must be noted before we speak of Jesus' Gospel, that the Bible, in particularly in Paul's writings, speaks of there being a *"Gospel of Christ"* (Romans 1:16) and *"Christ's Gospel"* (2Cor. 2:12). There is an important distinction that must be made in order to understand what is meant when we declare that we are preach or teaching the *"Gospel of Christ"*.

Generally speaking, the *Gospel of Christ* is the message that reveals Jesus' true identity as the Messiah and Savior that God promised. It is a message that tells *"about"* or *"of"* the life, Person and works of Jesus on the earth. This is the primary message (besides salvation) that the church has adopted and declared as *"the Gospel"*. Although this message provides insight into the identity of Christ, it does not communicate to us the whole message Jesus Himself brought as the provision of God to restore man in the earth.

On the other hand, *"Christ's Gospel"* is not a
message *about* the life of Christ, but is about the
message Christ Himself taught and delivered to
the church as the "good news" or Gospel. This is
where our attention must remain focused. We
cannot concentrate on the miracles and other
miraculous manifestations He wrought during
His life, without giving greater attention to what
He said. The miracles, signs and wonders was
not His message, but were given as support and
evidence that His message was genuine and
approved of by God.

Found within this message is the substance of
the divine plan of God and revelation of God's
provision for man's deliverance and restoration in
the earth. This is what the world is in need of –
deliverance and restoration. The Gospel of the
Kingdom contains the fullness of God's provision
for mankind to again reclaim his position and
fulfill his purpose in the earth.

There is probably not a more clear statement of what Jesus saw as His assignment and message than found in the Gospel of Luke when he said;

> *"I must preach the kingdom of God to other cities also: for therefore am I sent" (Luke 4:43).*

In addition, if were to open the very first book of the Gospels, the Book of Matthew, it would immediately discover what *"Christ's Gospel"* consisted of. In the Gospel of Matthew, we are told that Jesus' message concerned the Kingdom of God (Matthew 4:17, 23). As a matter of fact, you can hardly find a chapter within the book of Matthew where Jesus is not providing some form of instruction on the presence and reality of the Kingdom in the earth. If you were to remove the word Kingdom from Jesus' vocabulary you would be left with an incoherent and obviously incomplete message.

Before Jesus left the earth, He made it clear to His disciples what it was that they were to take

to the world as the Gospel. Specifically, He
commanded them:

> *"This gospel of the kingdom will be*
> *preached in all the world as a*
> *witness to all the nations, and then*
> *the end will come"* *(Matthew 24:14).*

Jesus specified *which* gospel was to be taught by
His emphatic use of the words *"this"*. The word
"this" specifically identifies and distinguishes *the*
Gospel of the Kingdom from other message that
we might label as gospels. Jesus, in turn
commanded the disciples that the Kingdom
should be their primary focus of their *prayers*
(Mat. 6:9-10), their *pursuit* in life (Mat. 6:33),
and the *message they preached* (Mat. 24:14, Luke
9:1, 10:1-9).

It cannot be overlooked, that Jesus considered
this message so important that He took time
after His resurrection to ensure that the church's
leadership clearly understood the Kingdom
message. Specifically, the Bible says:

*"To whom He also presented Himself
alive after His suffering by many
infallible proofs, being seen by them
during forty days and speaking of the
things pertaining to the kingdom of God"*
(Acts 1:3).

Wow! Jesus spent almost a month and a half
personally teaching the church's leadership on
the *"things pertaining to the kingdom of God"*. It
doesn't mention that He taught them on the Law,
Prophets, miracles, spiritual gifts, not even
salvation. He continued with the same message
He began His ministry teaching - the Kingdom
has arrived!

Philip's Gospel

The book of Acts chronicles the history of how the
church grew from a handful of believers to a
world shaking power. As seen in Acts 1:3, Jesus
spent 40 days instructing a handful of believers

with a message that possessed the power to transcend all social and economic distinctions, as well as to destroy the works of the kingdom of darkness. This power is demonstrated in the life and ministry of Phillip who was instructed in the Gospel Jesus delivered to the church at Jerusalem. In Acts chapter 8, the Bible records Philips trip to Samaria and the impact he had on this pagan city with the Gospel he had received. Specifically, the Bible records:

> "But there was a certain man called
> Simon, who previously practiced sorcery
> in the city and astonished the people of
> Samaria, claiming that he was someone
> great, to whom they all gave heed, from
> the least to the greatest, saying, "This
> man is the great power of God." And
> they heeded him because he had
> astonished them with his sorceries for a
> long time. But when they believed Philip
> as he preached the _things concerning
> the kingdom of God_ **and** the name of
> _Jesus Christ_, both men and women were
> baptized. Then Simon himself also
> believed; and when he was baptized he
> continued with Philip, and was amazed,
> seeing the miracles and signs which

were done (Acts 8:9-13) (bold and underline added).

The Gospel that Philip preached was not one of salvation alone, but one of power. The Bible describes the content of his message as being *<u>the things concerning the kingdom of God</u> and the name of Jesus Christ ..." This* is the same message described in Acts 1:3; where Jesus spent 40 days teaching those that were gathered in Jerusalem about the *"things concerning the Kingdom of God"*. Philip evidently was part of this group or received his instructions from someone who was present during Jesus' time of instruction.

As seen in the above referenced text, Philip was also instructed in the Person and power of the Name of Jesus the Christ. Philip presented the Full Gospel to the gentiles in Samaria, instructing them in both the Gospel of the Kingdom *<u>and</u>* Jesus Christ.

Paul's Gospel

Out of all of the New Testament writers, the Apostle Paul may be the most influential of them all. I say this due to the sheer volume of his writings and the impact that his pastoral epistles have had on the churches administration and doctrine. Taken as a whole, Paul is responsible for approximately two thirds of the New Testament.

Paul, having been educated by the very best in the law and Judaism, required a greater instructor than Gamaliel. Paul needed "The Master Instructor" to instruct him in the "new doctrine" that was abrasive to his Jewish doctrine and traditions. Therefore, Jesus Himself instructed Paul in the Gospel that He would take to the gentiles.

Christ, having blinded Paul on the Damascus Road, commissioned him to take the gospel to the

Gentiles. Shortly after receiving his sight Paul is said to have retreated into Arabia for 3 years before heading to Jerusalem to meet the apostles (Gal 1:16-24). I believe during his 3 year in Arabia that Jesus Himself personally instructed Paul to the things pertaining to the Kingdom just as He did with the other apostles in Acts 1:3 at the commencement of their ministries. For in the book of Galatians, Paul declares:

> *"But I make known to you, brethren, that the gospel which was preached by me is not according to man. For I neither received it from man, nor was I taught it, but it came through the revelation of Jesus Christ" (Galatians 1:11-12).*

In the Book of Acts, Paul specifically states what message he received and has gone about teaching when he said:

> *"And indeed, now I know that you all, among whom I have gone preaching the kingdom of God" (Acts 20:25).*

Like Philip, Paul preached and taught a Full Gospel. Specifically, the Bibles says:

> *"So when they had appointed him a day, many came to him at his lodging, to whom he explained and solemnly testified of <u>the kingdom of God</u>, persuading them <u>concerning Jesus</u> from both the Law of Moses and the Prophets, from morning till evening"* *(Acts 28:23) (underline added).*

Also,

> *Then Paul dwelt two whole years in his own rented house, and received all who came to him, preaching the <u>kingdom of God</u> **and** teaching the things which <u>concern the Lord Jesus Christ</u> with all confidence, no one forbidding him"* *(Acts 28:30-31)(underline and bold added).*

In both instances the Bible reveals that the content of Paul's message, like Philip's, consisted of instruction in the Kingdom first, then of Jesus as the Christ.

It appears from our study that the early church and Jesus Himself, considered the Gospel to be the revelation of:

(1) Access and presence of God's Kingdom, and

(2) Jesus the Messiah Christ and Savior.

Reclaiming the Power

A *kingdom-less* message is an incomplete message. It may have ability to initiate life, but lacks the power to transform and mature the believer's life. This is why there is so much disillusionment in the church. The church is not teaching the very thing the Word of God says that men are striving to possess and enter – the Kingdom (Luke 16:16). Men are seeking the rest and peace of God in their lives which comes from entering into the very thing He prepared for man in the very beginning.

This rest and fulfillment cannot be obtained by our efforts or religion, but by faith in Jesus, His finished work on the cross and our receiving

God's original and ultimate provision for man –
His Kingdom. As mentioned earlier, God worked
6 days in creating a Kingdom wherein man could
rule without having to worry about his needs
being met. In this environment, man's physical,
spiritual, mental and emotional needs were all
met by the God who made sure there were no
needs in His Kingdom. This is what the writer of
Hebrews meant when He wrote:

> *"For indeed the gospel was preached to
> us as well as to them; but the word
> which they heard did not profit them,
> not being mixed with faith in those who
> heard it. For we who have believed do
> enter that rest, as He has said: "So I
> swore in My wrath, 'They shall not enter
> My rest,'" although the works were
> finished from the foundation of the
> world. For He has spoken in a certain
> place of the seventh day in this way:
> "And God rested on the seventh day
> from all His works" ... 'There remains
> therefore a rest for the people of God.
> For he who has entered His rest has
> himself also ceased from his works as
> God did from His. Let us therefore be
> diligent to enter that rest, lest anyone*

fall according to the same example of
disobedience" (Hebrews 4:2-4, 9-11).

When man's soul cannot find what it desires, and
that which the Word of God promises, it grows
weary and the individual eventually faints; or
they all together fall away from the faith. This is
unacceptable!

This is why the Gospel of the Kingdom must be
restored in the church and the Full Gospel must
be preached! Without the Full Gospel of the
Kingdom, the believer and the church are ill-
equipped to experience victory against a ferocious
enemy. The Full Gospel offers the souls of men
rest from their toil and efforts to find fulfillment
in this world. It provides them with the power to
overcome the enemy that comes to oppress and
defeat them (see Matthew 6:25-33, Luke 11:20).

The church can never truly enter into that place
of rest and victory until it returns to its

foundation and reclaim the power that Christ delivered to the church for its victory. The Gospel of the Kingdom is not another doctrine or message, but the provision God to advance His rule, reign and way of doing things in the earth.

The apostle Paul said it best when he declared:

> *"For the kingdom of God is not in word but in power."*
> *1 Corinthians 4:20*

FULL GOSPEL

KINGDOM SCRIPTURE REFERENCE

JOHN'S THE BAPTIST GOSPEL

Mat 3:2
Luke 16:16a

JESUS' GOSPEL

Mat 4:17
Mat 4:23
Mat 5:3, 10, 19-20
Mat 6:10, 13
Mat 6:33
Mat 7:21
Mat 8:11, 12
Mat 9:35
Mat 11:11, 12
Mat 12:25, 26, 28
Mat 13:11, 19, 24, 31, 33, 38, 41-47, 52
Mat 16:19, 28
Mat 18:1-4, 23
Mat 19:12, 14, 23-24
Mat 20:1, 21, 31, 43
Mat 22:2
Mat 23:13
Mat 24:1-7, 14
Mat 25:1, 14, 34,
Mat 26:29
Mar 10:23-25
*Mar 12:34
Luke 1:33, See also Isaiah 9:6-7
Luke 4:43
Luke 9:2, 11, 27
Luke 9:60, 62

Luke 12:32
Luke 13:28-29
Luke 16:16
Luke 17:20-21
Luke 18:16-17, 24-29
Luke 19:11-15
Luke 21:31
Luke 22:16-18
Luke 22:29
John 3:3-5
John 18:36
Act 1:3

THE DISCIPLES' GOSPEL:

Mat 10:7
Luke 10:9-11
Act 1:3
Act 8:12

PHILIP GOSPEL

Acts 8:12

APOLLOS GOSPEL

Acts 18:24-28

PAUL'S GOSPEL

Act 19:8
Act 20:25
Act 28:23
Act 28:31

FULL GOSPEL

FULL GOSPEL

About the Author

Dr. J.C. Matthews is the Senior Pastor of Dunamis Life Ministries and founder of J.C. Matthews Ministries, REIGN Publications a.k.a. Blessed Books Publishing Company, the International Kingdom Institute, REIGN Worldwide Inc, and the REIGN Worldwide International Fellowship of Churches. J.C. and wife Gena also host the Kingdom teaching television programs "Living Life Powerfully" and "The EMBASSY".

J.C. has worked for some of America's top corporations prior to entering into full time ministry. Dr. Matthews possesses a B.A in Political Science, as well as a Juris Doctorate (J.D.) degree. In addition, J.C. was twice recognized (1996 and 1997) for the outstanding study of law by the "Who's Who Among American Law Students" and was also honored as an Urban All-American by the General Assembly of the Ohio State Senate.

www.drjcmatthews.com

FULL GOSPEL

Additional Resources from

J.C. Matthews & REIGN Worldwide Inc.

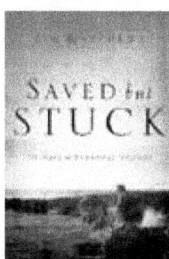

For more information visit: www.reignworldwide.org

FULL GOSPEL

FULL GOSPEL